BUDDHISM AND ZEN

Buddhism and Zen

Compiled, Edited and Translated
by
NYOGEN SENZAKI
and
RUTH STROUT McCANDLESS

PHILOSOPHICAL LIBRARY
NEW YORK

Ph.1
76172
JUL 25 '55

BL
1442
Z4
S47

53-7898
8-8-55

0698

FOREWORD

It is now a number of years since I first met the Zen Buddhist monk, Nyogen Senzaki. By that time I had read scriptures and commentaries of several religions and many sects in my quest for information, and was familiar with the writings of Dr. D. T. Suzuki, whose analysis of Zen and translations of its literature held especial interest. In following this interest in an elusive and little known phase of Buddhism, I met Mr. Senzaki, who passed his days in comparative obscurity translating from old manuscripts and talking with visitors. As time passed, I was allowed to copy the work he had done as well as work with him on some of the current translations.

This book contains a few of the shorter and more simple of the translations together with comments to elucidate their meaning, and a few notes on the principles and practice of Zen given to students.

To the best of our knowledge there is no material available at present for a beginner. The notes in this book have been gathered and arranged as an elementary introduction to Zen Buddhism as well as a practical guide to its further understanding.

RUTH STROUT McCANDLESS

Pasadena, California

The Buddha-body is omnipresent.
Each sentient being beholds it
Through aspiration and Karma relation
As it dwells eternally on this seat of meditation.*

* It is the inherent nature of the Buddha-body that it individualizes itself in myriad manifestations in the phenomenal world. It does not stand alone outside particular existences, but abides in them, animates them, and makes them move freely. In this form it is subjected to certain conditions such as time, space and causation. Its essence is infinite, but its manifestations are finite and limited. It is for this reason that the Buddha-body has to wait until conditions are matured before expressing itself.

Suppose that there is a mirror . . . the mirror of the Buddha-body. Anything that comes in front of it is reflected without any premeditation on the part of the mirror. Beautiful or ugly, high or low, rich or poor, good or evil, everything is reflected impartially. Wherever and whenever conditions are correct, all particular things will be reflected in the mirror or Mind-Essence of the Buddha-body without hesitation, without reasoning, without demonstration. It is thus that the principle of Karma works.

Although things are many and subject to constant transformation and regulation by their Karma, the Buddha-body abides eternally on the seat of Bodhi, our inmost being.

The moon is shining serenely in the sky, casting her reflection in countless places wherever conditions are matured. We see her image on the least trace of water or a vast expanse, which may be polluted or clean, but each reflects the same moon according to its nature. The shadows also are as numerous as the bodies of water, but we cannot say that one shadow is essentially different from another, nor has the moon left her orbit even for a moment.

CONTENTS

BUDDHISM AND ZEN

INTRODUCTION

Buddhism was already established in China when Bodhi-Dharma arrived from India in the Sixth Century. Monasteries had been built, many of the Sutras[1] translated, and learned students of Buddhism spent long hours discoursing upon the nuances of the religious and philosophical aspects of its teachings. A thousand years had passed since Buddha's death. In India the two major schools of Buddhism, the Hinayana and the Mahayana,[2] were developing according to their principles. The Hinayana, or Lesser Vehicle, basing its premise on the Pali texts, clung to the letter of the Sutras without regard for one of Buddha's primary tenets, namely, that all is constant change. The Mahayana, or Greater Vehicle, taught not only the necessity for enlightenment, but also the need to stay in the world to enlighten others. The Hinayanists had kept their school pure, but at the expense of growth, whereas the Mahayanists had grown, but often at the expense of purity of understanding. In both schools Buddhist teachings were sometimes obscured by the earlier beliefs and superstitions of its converts.

Chinese Buddhism was predominately Mahayana, and, at this date, more concerned with the precepts than with enlightenment. China's own great teachers, Kung-fu-tsu and Lao-tzu, had many adherents. Confucianism was of more popular appeal because it laid down definite rules and regulations to be followed, but Taoism had deep roots among the more intellectual. When the grad-

[1] Sutra . . . a Buddhist scripture (Sutra: Sanskrit; Sutta: Pali.)
[2] Hinayana and Mahayana are names used by the Mahayanists to designate the two main schools of Buddhism. Although they differ in point of view, they are united as Buddhists.

3

ual spread of Buddhism began in China around 200 A.D., it found fertile ground in both Confucianism and Taoism. Confucianists appreciated Buddhist ethics, and Taoists understood the ultimate aim of Buddhism. As Chinese scholars translated the Sanskrit texts of the *Tripitaka*[3] available to them, they automatically stripped off some of the more fanciful flights of Indian philosophy in favor of the practical approach demanded by their own nature. The Chinese had little use for abstract theory unrelated to practical application.

Bodhi-Dharma, the "Blue-eyed Monk," and twenty-eighth successor of Buddha Sakyamuni,[4] had not made the long journey to involve himself in academic discussion nor to curry favor among the famous. When he was brought before the emperor, the emperor recited his own numerous charities, which included the building and endowing of monasteries, then asked Bodhi-Dharma what credit he had so achieved. Much to the emperor's surprise, Bodhi-Dharma replied, "None whatever."

Those who followed Bodhi-Dharma were young men of great determination dedicated to complete enlightenment. Bodhi-Dharma did not encourage them, but when they had proved their sincerity, he taught them and meditated with them. Hui-k'e was the first in China to receive the "Lamp of Dharma," of which Bodhi-Dharma said:

"A special transmission outside the scriptures;
Without dependence on words or letters;
Direct pointing to the essence of mind;
Seeing one's true nature and attaining Buddhahood."

Bodhi-Dharma foretold that "with five petals the flower would be complete." Succeeding generations produced five outstanding

[3] Tripitaka . . . literally, "Three Baskets," containing all the Buddhist scriptures.

[4] Buddha Sakyamuni . . . the same as Gautama Buddha.

teachers, from whose particular methods five Chinese Zen schools were evolved continuing the teaching and transmitting the Dharma.

These schools were known as the *Dhyana*[5] or Meditation schools. *Ch'an,* the Chinese equivalent of *Dhyana,* became *Zen* when introduced in Japan in the twelfth century. Japanese scholars wrote the first books in English on the subject, and it is for this reason that the Western world now uses the word *Zen* in its religio-philosophical vocabulary. *Zen* originally meant meditation, but it came to mean also enlightenment, the means of enlightenment, concentration of mind, and even certain qualities for which Zen followers became noted.

The teachings of the Sixth Patriarch, Wei Lang (Hui-neng, Eno or Yeno), were gathered into a Sutra becoming known as the *Chinese Sutra,* the only one outside the translated portions of the *Tripitaka.* This Sutra is based on Buddhism, but it is interesting to note that early writers seldom mentioned Zen or even Buddhism by name, writing only of principles and practice.

Zen grew out of Buddhism and Taoism, and has for centuries been a distinct, unique form of Buddhism. Zen does not claim that only those of Buddhist background and training can achieve its realization. When Meister Eckhart asserted, "The eye with which I see God is the same eye with which God sees me," Zen nodded its agreement. It willingly accepts all that is true in any religion and recognizes those of any faith who have gained complete realization; however, it knows that despite great sincerity a person, whose religious training is based on dualism, will have an unnecessarily difficult time before gaining enlightenment. Zen brushes aside anything, no matter of what seeming triviality, that does not deal directly with reality, nor will it countenance anything less than an individual's own experience. Does a student cling to the Sutras? They are worthless scraps of paper!

[5] *Dhyana* . . . Sanskrit for meditation.

Does a student depend on Buddha? Who is that fellow? Does a student claim he carries nothing with him? Then drop it! The ko-an[6] was devised as a means of driving the student to an impasse that could not be solved by the intellect, thereby forcing him to abandon all forms of dualism and theory to deal with the problem directly.

No one can describe enlightenment to another. To perceive it one must achieve it for himself. It is easy enough to say what Zen is not, but to say what Zen is is another matter entirely.

Zen has come down to the present time in a direct line, generation after generation. Although it is transmitted directly, it has nothing to do with "teaching and learning." The Lamp of Dharma can be received only by those who have fulfilled the conditions for its reception. A teacher may point the way or help to guide a student, but the work, like the accomplishment, is the student's.

Zen cannot be adulterated. The moment there is a trace to be perceived, it is no longer Zen. It is for this reason that there are so few true teachers. In recent years monks have left the monasteries to set themselves up as priests, supported by the parish, answerable to a hierarchy within the sect, and even establishing their own households near the temple grounds. Too lazy to provide for themselves, and too dishonest to admit it, they yet profess to lead others to enlightenment! It cannot be done. Zen will continue quietly on its way, avoiding organizations, sectarianism, or any other restriction. In the West there are people who use the name of Zen to attract followers. Zen never advertises itself. Other religions may approve of students who are eager to spread the teachings, but Buddhism discourages proselyting. To Bud-

[6] Ko-an . . . derived from Chinese, *kung-an*. A problem given to the student for solution, the answer to which cannot be reached intellectually. Ko-an originally signified a public announcement, and there are monasteries today that employ it as a part of their displayed ritual; such a practice is, however, frowned upon by those who have achieved enlightenment.

dhists perseverance means inner culture rather than outer growth. "Silence speaks a million words, and a million words express nothing but silence."

When we "gain the meaning," each moment of each day enlightenment will be actualized. As Soyen Shaku once said, "What is philosophical in Buddhism is no more than a preliminary step toward what is practical in it."

R. S. McC.

TEN QUESTIONS

Buddhism is no longer considered a strange teaching filled with superstition and idol worship, but is now understood by the intellectual people of the world as a religion of enlightenment entirely in accord with the latest findings of science and the highest of ethical culture. With the increase of Western interest in Buddhism has come the desire for exact, uncolored information on the subject. Philologists may translate the scriptures and commentaries faithfully, but, without a deeper understanding of their meaning, the words can be misleading or without significance. Priests from the temples are often anxious to increase the membership of their congregations, so we find them stressing outward conformity at the price of inner development. It is an accepted fact that all major religions have been altered and many of their concepts distorted by those whose lives were allegedly dedicated to the continuation and dissemination of their teachings. Also, religions have been colored by the earlier beliefs and practices indigenous to varying peoples.

Buddhism is divided into two groups often referred to as *Hinayana* and *Mahayana*. In general the difference may be described as retiring from the world to seek enlightenment for oneself, and remaining in the world to enlighten oneself and others. Although there are sects within each of these groups, all are united in the basic teachings as given by Gautama Buddha.

The following ten questions are those most frequently asked by non-Buddhists:

What does a Buddhist believe or worship?

The words "believe" and "worship" are unfamiliar to Buddhists because they do not "believe" but understand, and they do not "worship" but practice what they understand.

Is Buddha an Oriental god?

The answer is a definite, "No." Buddha was a human being, a student of philosophy and a seeker of ultimate truth. He was born Gautama Siddhartha, crown prince of Nepal, 565 years before the Christian era. When he was twenty-nine years old, he renounced his position to become a mendicant monk, and, after six years of hard work, he became enlightened through his meditation. He then travelled and taught among the people of India for forty-five years. His teachings were recorded in Sanskrit and Pali, and later translated into Chinese, Japanese and other Asiatic languages. At the present time only about nine percent of these scriptures have been translated into Western languages. English philologists and archeologists did much of the early work of translating, then the Germans, French and Scandinavians followed with books in their own tongues. American students, who are more interested in the spirit of Buddhism and the practical application of the teachings, now have two main currents of Buddhist thought from which to draw . . . the Oriental and Occidental.

On his death bed Buddha said, "The teachings I have given you will be your teacher when I am gone." He called the whole system of his teachings, *Dharma* or *Dhamma*, the law of the universe. Buddhism is a teaching that will free our minds to come into harmony with this universal law. As such, this teaching is gradually becoming the invisible treasure of intellectual people the world over.

If Buddha is not a god, then there must be a real god above us.
Do Buddhists believe in a god?

If you use the word "God" as a poetical expression of universal law, then the answer is, yes. If you imply by the term some personal existence apart from universal law, then the answer is, no. Buddhists understand the universe and God as one. There is no remainder in the mathematics of infinity. All life is one, therefore, there cannot be God and man nor a universe and God. A god not in the world is a false god, and a world not in God is unreal. All things return to one, and one operates in all.

It does not follow that just because a person does not believe in a personal god he is a heathen or unmoral. On the contrary he may know the true nature of man and the universe better than more orthodox followers of younger religions. Buddhists left anthropomorphic ideas behind twenty-five centuries ago.

If there is no god outside this world, who created the world?

If you are so attached to the word "God," then the universe is God and God is the universe. To say that God created the universe, and then to say that he stands outside this universe is a contradiction. Neither God nor no-God can exist outside this oneness. Early Christians understood this better, but later people with less understanding placed a god outside the universe. In other words, they created God. We create the world each moment of each day. When we are asleep, there is nothing, but once we are awake, then the world of form, color, odor, taste and touch are instantly created by our senses. Buddhists see the world as a phenomenon of flux consisting of various relations, but not created by some divinity. Einstein brought the concept of relativity to scientific knowledge, since proved in the laboratories of the world.

This world is conceived in the relation of both subjectivity and objectivity. Buddha concluded that without this relationship of the world to the elements, subjective and objective, there is nothing. If you think that this world is created by a supreme being, then you must feel that you are powerless to change anything, thus leaving your fate to the mercy of that creator. Buddhists know that the world is your own production. You may change it, rebuild it or improve it to suit your own will.

Then what is mind? Was not this mind given by God at the very beginning?

Judge fairy tales or legends for yourself. If there is no personal God, then no one but you can create the mind. The mind is an endless chain of three processes; namely, craving, acting and discontent. These three make a cycle . . . craving to acting, acting to discontent, and discontent to craving again. Without these three processes there is no mind and, consequently, no body. When this point of view is expanded, it will be seen that everything in the universe operates according to these processes, under the law of causation, and aside from this endless chain there is no creator, no ruler of the universe. Buddhism places the center of the universe in the subjectivity of individual mind, whereas other religions put it in the objectivity outside the individual mind.

What is the first cause, the very beginning of everything?

Some religions answer God, Allah, Brahma, or something outside the individual. Buddhism sweeps aside your idle speculation and tells you to find the answer in your own realization. Your intellection will not solve the problem, but will use your time to push the solution farther from you. Buddhism does not ask you to believe that you yourself are the creator, nor to accept the proposition that you are not making vicarious atonement for the transgressions of another, but it does promise that when you have fulfilled the requirements, you will know the answer beyond the shadow of a doubt.

Do Buddhists believe in a future life?

Yes, if you mean the continuation of cosmic life, but, no, if you mean a later individual life. We are living in an endless world, the world of karmic life or the world of three processes. Other religions teach that your life comes to an end and you receive judgment, but Buddhism teaches that good character or bad character continues according to individual desire. In other religions past, present and future are set in a straight line, but to Buddhists they are mere names for an endless circle.

Does the word BUDDHA ever signify anything other than the man who proclaimed these teachings?

Yes. Buddha means an enlightened mental state or condition. Often in writings on Buddhism the term means this alone. Gautama Siddhartha was called Buddha because he attained supreme knowledge and moral perfection through his own perseverance, but he was neither a god revealing himself to mankind nor one sent by a god to bring salvation to the world. He attained his realization through his own striving without seeking help from a god or man. Although Buddhists refer to Gautama Siddhartha as Buddha, they also recognize other Buddhas both before and since his time. Buddhahood is the goal of our culture, which anyone can attain, but there is by no means any saving power to it unless we save ourselves. There is no savior outside the brilliancy of enlightened wisdom.

If you have a figure or picture of Buddha in your home, do not worship it nor pray to it for fortune or health. Keep it as a reminder of your own future being. As you learn meditation the calm poise depicted will be your good companion. Bear in mind Buddha's words, "If you try to see me through my form, or if you try to hear me through my voice, you will never reach me and will remain forever a stranger to my teaching."

Are there precepts in Buddhism comparable to the Ten Commandments or the Sermon on the Mount?

Yes. Buddhist monks and nuns keep more than two hundred and fifty precepts. The *Brahmajala Sutra* lists ten precepts for all Mahayana Buddhists to keep. American Buddhists keep three precepts: *first,* to avoid all evil thoughts and evil actions; *second,* to attain good thoughts and right actions; *third,* to develop *Prajna*[1] so that all humanity is benefited and all sentient beings mercifully treated.

From these precepts it follows naturally that no living thing is killed for individual pleasure, there is loving-kindness for all sentient beings; nothing is taken which does not belong to one . . . live an unselfish and generous life; in marriage keep constancy strictly with love and respect for each other . . . purify and refine yourself; speak no word that is not true . . . develop integrity in every way; avoid intoxication and lead a pure and sober life . . . keep yourself clean and worthy.

What is the attitude of Buddhism toward other religions?

"Buddhism has no destructive intention against other religions. This is the distinctive mark by which Buddhist missionary work is differentiated from the work of Christian and Moslem missionaries. The Christian-Moslem view has usually been that destruction must precede construction, or at any rate, that the two must go hand in hand. The Buddhist aim has been, usually, to do no destroying and to put all its emphasis on the constructive and positive side."[2] There is no blood stain on the history of Buddhist

---

[1] Prajna . . . Sanskrit: wisdom . . . that quality of ability to see directly into the true nature of things beyond mere intellection.

[2] James Bissett Pratt, Ph.D.—*The Pilgrimage of Buddhism.* Macmillan Co., 1928.

proselyting. In no instance have they tried to destroy the customs of other faiths or countries by ridicule or force, neither do they insist on the exclusive use of their own rituals or rites. They accept what is true and beautiful in every religion, and they study the scriptures and teachings of all faiths. Buddhism is spread by the quiet influence of those who live its teachings day by day, and through the information given in universities, colleges and libraries all over the world.

NOTES ON MEDITATION

Although the word *Zen* is derived from the Chinese transliteration of the Sanskrit *Dhyana*,[1] it is not the same as *Dhyana*. Dai-to once said, "One may pass hours sitting in contemplation, but if he has no Zen, he is not my disciple." On another occasion a student came to Kwan-Zan to receive personal guidance. Kwan-Zan asked him where he had studied Zen and under which master. When the student replied that he had studied under Jaku-shitsu of Yo-gen Monastery, Kwan-Zan said, "Show me what you have learned." The student's answer was to sit cross-legged in silence, whereupon Kwan-Zan shouted, "My monastery has too many stone Buddhas. We need no more. Get out, you good-for-nothing!"

Zen uses meditation as a means of entering *Samadhi*,[2] but it does not deny the existence of other methods; however, it does insist that what is gained by the practice of Za-zen[3] must be practically applied in everyday life. The teachings of Zen warn constantly of falling into the trap of "quietism."

When one devotes himself to meditation, his mental burdens, unnecessary worries and wandering thoughts drop off one by one; he feels that things go smoothly and somewhat pleasantly. A

[1] Dhyana . . . Sanskrit: meditation.
[2] Samadhi . . . Sanskrit: is sometimes used in place of dhyana, but more often is referred to as that condition achieved by the practice of dhyana.
[3] Za-zen . . . from Chinese, *tso ch'an,* to sit in meditation.

student may now depend on his intuition to make decisions. As he moves "at first glance," second thought with its dualism, doubt and hesitation, does not arise.

Consciousness is not an entity ruling the movements of the mind, but a focus of mental powers. When mental activities cease working in meditation, there is no focus, but the moment the five senses begin to work, consciousness flares up immediately. It is exactly the same when a person goes to sleep; there is nothing unusual or strange about it.

Sometimes beginners in meditation speak about their dreams as though there was some connection between Zen realization and dreaming. Dreams are a psychological phenomenon and have nothing to do with Zen.

Ko-an

A ko-an is a problem given by a teacher to the student for solution. The student must solve it himself, although a teacher will occasionally give him some help. To work upon a ko-an, your eagerness for its solution is necessary; to solve a ko-an, you must face it without thinking of it. The more you pound it in cognition, the more difficult its solution will become. Two hands brought together produce a sound. What is the sound of one hand? This is a ko-an. If you think that there is no such sound, you are giving up your privilege.

A Zen ko-an is nothing but nonsense to outsiders, but for a student it is a gate to Zen. Intellectual gymnastics, no matter how superior or refined, can never solve a ko-an; in fact, it is given to force a student beyond intellection. Do not work upon more than one ko-an at a time, and do not discuss a ko-an with any person other than your teacher. Just face the question without thinking anything else. Do not neglect your duties of everyday life, but use any leisure moment of the mind for the ko-an.

Each ko-an is an expression of a person's actual experience, directly from his attainment. When you reach the same stage, you will express the same thing. Unless you attain realization for yourself, it is useless for philosophers or spiritual teachers to talk about noumenon, oneness, the absolute, God within you or any other empty name, which will only serve to lead you astray.

Unless you have faith in being enlightened in this life, you had better not study Zen at all. There are plenty of sects promising enlightenment after death . . . go to them and be happy.

Before you enter one of the gates of Zen, you must strip yourself of egoistic ideas. If you think you can reason out the final truth with your brain, why do you not do it? Once you begin your work on Zen, do not turn to the left nor to the right but keep going straight ahead.

Eki-do, a Zen master of Japan, who lived in the nineteenth century, made the following vows: first, the cascade of life and death must be crossed over. (What is life? What is death? These problems must be solved clearly.) Until the dawn of such a realization, I will not stop my meditation. Second, every hour in the day and every hour in the night I will try to live as Buddhas and patriarchs lived. Their way is untransmissible and can be attained only by living. Third, from eternity to eternity my life is endless. Wherever I am, whenever I live, I should not have any secondary thought for environment, favorable or adverse.

The average man does not know the true meaning of life and death, so he clings to life and is afraid of death. A Bodhisattva does not hold his body as his own, nor does he see mind and body as two separate things. When he recognizes it by the senses, he calls it body, when he sees it by introspection, he names it mind. Most people cling to "their" thoughts, thus causing suffering in the world. In the *Diamond Sutra,* Buddha said, "In case good men and women raise the desire for supreme enlightenment, they should thus keep their thoughts under control. If a Bodhisattva[4] retains the thought of an ego, a person, a being, or a soul, he is no more a Bodhisattva." My logic can convince your reason, but I cannot overcome the inertia of your dualistic thinking. Your intellect may comprehend the oneness of all things, but your thinking, like a cascade, will continue to flow in dualism. You must cross this cascade once for all to see for yourself the true emptiness of which Buddha said, "All that has form is an illusive existence. When it is perceived that all form is no-form, the Tathagata[5] is recognized."

"Every hour in the day and every hour in the night I will try to live as Buddhas and patriarchs lived." Buddhism does not seek adherents. If you desire worldly fame in any form, then work for that instead of hiding yourself under the name of "Buddhist." "Their way is untransmissible . . ." live the life and you will know. When Zen says, "Dharma was transmitted from a teacher to a disciple," it means only that the disciple perceived enlighten-ment himself, thereby "receiving the Lamp of Dharma."

"I should not have any secondary thought for environment." Do not try to cling to your pleasures. It is as impossible as at-tempting to catch sunshine in a box. Do not stop your tears. It will not help you to ask why you are sad. Avoid secondary thought. All things are transient, your happiness as well as your

[4] Bodhisattva . . . a person dedicated not only to his own enlightenment but also to the enlightenment of all sentient beings, and in this way distinct from *Arhat.*

[5] Tathagata . . . Buddha . . . Mind Essence . . . Eternal Presence . . . Eternal Now.

sorrow, and secondary thoughts will bring you nothing but suffering.

> The bamboo shadows are sweeping the stairs,
> But no dust is stirred.
> The moonlight penetrates the depths of the pool,
> But no trace is left in the water.

❖❖❖❖❖❖❖❖

Emptiness

Emptiness is a term used in Buddhism that has caused considerable misunderstanding in Western minds. When a Buddhist speaks of emptiness, he does not intend it to signify the opposite of fullness, but rather that unconditioned state in which there is nothing to be given and nothing to be received. Since it cannot be expressed in speech, it can only be hinted at in dialogue or referred to by use of the word "emptiness."

Some students have advanced far enough in their meditation to empty their minds, but once they resume their normal activity, they are as unstable as before. In effect they continue a condition of mind in which they recognize that there is nothing, not realizing that this in itself is a concrete, self-limiting state quite different from the "emptiness" of Buddhism.

True emptiness cannot be included nor excluded. When you count your inhalations and exhalations, contending thoughts will gradually disappear leaving no trace. Meditation? Forget it. Emptiness? Forget it. Realization? Forget it. Buddha? Forget that fellow. Your everyday life will become calm and contented, making you less talkative, less worried, and less excitable. At a glance you will recognize your true self.

❖❖❖❖❖❖❖❖

Karma

Karma is a Sanskrit noun in the nominative case derived from the verb, Kar, meaning to do; in the objective case it is Karman.

Kamma and *Kamman* are the Pali equivalents. All states and conditions in this life are the direct results of previous actions, and each action in the present determines the fate of the future. Life is the working process of *Karman,* the endless series of cause and effect.

In the *Dhammapada,* Buddha said: "All that is, is the result of thought, it is founded on thought, it is made of thought. If a man speaks or acts with an evil thought, pain follows him, as the wheel follows the foot of the ox that draws the carriage. All that is, is the result of thought, it is founded on thought, it is made of thought. If a man speaks or acts with a pure thought, happiness follows him, like a shadow that never leaves him."

Buddhism teaches the way to emancipation and enlightenment, but Gautama Buddha never suggested that the way to perfection was easy or simple. Before he achieved his own enlightenment, he experienced tremendous difficulties. The natural tendency of every man is toward ease, comfort, and the "good" things of life, but if he wants to climb the upward path, he must toil hard. His aspiration for perfection must be accomplished by self-discipline. Deliverance is not to be attained by prayer, belief in creeds, nor initiation into secret orders or mysteries, but by leading an upright, worthy life. Purification is accomplished by being conscious of every thought, word and act, and, by the avoidance of evil to respect life. To respect life is to practice the ordinary virtues, to be honest, to live cleanly and think purely, to be just and kind, to respect others and to live in peace with them, and to strive against ignorance.

Buddha is a state of mind . . . intellectual and moral perfection. It means enlightenment; one who is truly enlightened is a Buddha. Buddha Sakyamuni attained Buddhahood through his own efforts, and declared that it was possible for anyone to do the same. By his own efforts each must find his inner treasure and see it for himself.

Bodhi-Dharma once said, "If you wish to see the Buddha, you must look into your own inner-nature; this nature is the Buddha himself. If you have not seen your own nature, what is the use of thinking of Buddha, or reciting Sutras, or fasting, or keeping the precepts? By thinking of Buddha, your meritorious deed will bear fruit; by reciting the Sutras, you may attain a bright intellect; by keeping the precepts, you may be born into the heavens; by practicing charity, you may be rewarded abundantly; but as to seeking the Buddha, you are far away."

❖❖❖❖❖❖❖

The Practice of Meditation

Truth is perfect and complete in itself. It is not something just newly discovered . . . it has always existed.

Truth is not far away; it is ever near. Do not try to walk to it because your every step leads not away from it.

Do not follow some other person's thoughts, but learn to listen to the voice within yourself. Your body and your mind will blend in unity, and you will realize the oneness of all life.

Even a delicate movement of your dualistic thought will prevent you from entering Samadhi, the Palace of Meditation.

Those who talk much about realization are usually wandering outside its gates, and will have some struggle before they enter this Palace of Meditation.

Buddha Sakyamuni meditated six years, and Bodhi-Dharma meditated nine years. The practice of meditation is not a method for the attainment of realization but is enlightenment itself.

Your search among books, word upon word, may lead you to the depths of the cognition world, but it is not the way to receive the reflection of your true self.

When you have thrown off your ideas as to mind and body, you will see the original man in full. Zen is nothing but the actualization of truth; therefore, the longings which are followed by actions are not the true attitude of Zen at all.

To attain the blessedness of meditation you should begin the practice with a pure motive and a firm determination. Your room for meditation must be clean and quiet. Take your regular meal sparingly, and shut out all noises and disturbances. Do not let the mind dwell in thought on what is good or what is bad. Just relax and forget that you are meditating. Do not desire to become a Buddha. If you do, you will never become one.

Sit down in a chair with a large cushion in a manner as comfortable as possible. Wear the clothing loosely, and remove your shoes, but keep your feet in a pair of warm slippers.

Put your right hand on your left thigh, palm up, and let it hold the four fingers of your left hand so that the left thumb may press down the right thumb. Hold your body straight. Lean not to the left nor the right. Do not tip forward nor bend to the back. Your ears should be at right angles to your shoulders, and your nose must be on a straight line with the navel. Keep your tongue at the roof of your mouth and close your lips and teeth firmly. Keep your eyes slightly open, and breathe through your nostrils.

Before you begin meditation, move your body from right to left a few times, then take several slow, deep breaths. Hold your body erect, allowing your breathing to become normal again. Many thoughts will crowd into your mind . . . just ignore them and they will soon vanish. Do not allow the mind to become negative, or you will fall asleep. Think that which you cannot think. In other words, think nothing. This is the proper way to meditate according to Zen teaching.

Zen meditation is not physical culture, nor is it a method to gain something material. It is peacefulness and blessedness itself.

It is the actualization of Buddha-Dharma,[6] namely, the ultimate truth of universal oneness.

In your meditation you yourself are the mirror reflecting the solution of your problems. The human mind has absolute freedom within its true nature. You can attain your emancipation intuitively. Do not work for emancipation . . . but allow the work itself to be emancipation.

When you wish to rest, move your body slowly and stand up quietly. Practice this meditation in the morning, or in the evening, or at any leisure time during the day. You will soon then realize that your mental burdens are dropping away from you one by one, and that you are gaining a sort of intuitive power hitherto unnoticed. Do not think that the wise do not need to meditate. The wise and the dull should both take time for meditation. Constant practice of mind culture will lead anyone to the realization of truth.

In Oriental countries there have been thousands upon thousands of students who have practiced Zen meditation and obtained its fruits. Do not doubt its possibilities because of the simplicity of its method. If you cannot find the truth right where you are, where else do you expect to wander in finding it?

Life is short and no one knows what the next moment will bring. Cultivate your mind while you have the opportunity, thereby gaining the treasures of wisdom, which in turn you can share abundantly with others, bringing them happiness.

— Dō-gen (1200-1253)

✦✦✦✦✦✦✦✦

Each one of us should try to be the master of his own mind and body, to govern his environment peacefully, to lead a pure

6 Buddha-Dhamma . . . Pali; Buddha-Dharma . . . Sanskrit: enlightened wisdom.

and unselfish life, and to be kind and helpful to all fellow beings. These are our most important daily tasks.

Zen Buddhism is the vehicle of *Buddha Hrydaya*,[7] the brilliancy of enlightenment, the highest and most essential of all teaching. This enlightenment is not confined to hermitages in remote mountains; it transcends all customs, all sects, all life, all places and all time, and is as applicable in the busy city as in the quiet country.

As to the place where you meditate, as well as the conditions for its practice and continuance, there are ten essential requirements:

1. For beginners the place should be clean and quiet.
2. Its temperature should be comfortable during all seasons.
3. It should be well ventilated.
4. Beginners should not meditate when the weather is either too warm or too cold.
5. The place should be neither too dark nor too light.
6. It should not offer any view that distracts the mind.
7. Beginners in meditation should avoid association with men of fame or with those who like to argue.
8. Beginners in meditation should avoid association with those who like competitive games.
9. Beginners in meditation should avoid all places of danger such as fire, flood, storm and the haunts of criminals.
10. Beginners should not meditate by the sea nor in the vicinity of pleasure resorts.

There are ten things about the physical condition to be guarded while you are learning how to meditate:

1. Your stomach should be neither empty nor full.
2. Dress comfortably in clean clothes, but never be greedy for fine clothing.

---

[7] Buddha-Hrydaya . . . brilliancy of enlightenment.

3. Regulate your hours for sleep.
4. Keep your leisure hours for meditation.
5. Do not waste your time writing poems or essays on Zen.
6. Do not meditate immediately after meals.
7. Do not try to meditate when you are too nervous.
8. If possible, remove the shoes while meditating.
9. Bathe daily.
10. A healthy body means healthy meditation. First of all, take care of your health.

There are ten things you should know about your mind as you learn meditation:

1. Do not think of either good or bad nor of right and wrong.
2. Do not think of either the past or the future. The present moment should contain your entire universe during meditation.
3. Do not be ambitious to attain realization. Do not desire to become a Buddha.
4. Both before and after meditation think of *Anicca*, impermanency; think also of *Anatta*, the impossibility of identifying any self entity in either your mind or your body.
5. Do not cling to subjectivity; do not cling to objectivity. Non-thinking and non-clinging purify the mind.
6. Before and after meditation repeat your vow to save all sentient beings.*
7. When your mind wanders, clasp your hands tightly, or concentrate upon the tip of your nose. Usually awareness of the lower part of your abdomen prevents mind-wandering.
8. If you feel dizzy during meditation, concentrate your mind upon your forehead.

* The Bodhisattva's Vow:
 However innumerable sentient beings may be, I vow to save them all;
 However inexhaustible the evil passions are, I vow to destroy them;
 However immeasurable the sacred teachings are, I vow to learn them all;
 No matter how difficult the path of Buddhahood may be,
   I vow to follow it to the end.

9. If you feel sick, concentrate your mind upon your toes. (Zen students should keep their minds upon their feet when walking.)

10. Without moving or holding anything in your mind, or clinging either to a positive or negative idea, advance step by step ahead in your meditation until you hear the sound of one hand.

—Some items translated
from Kei-Zan (1268-1325)

❖❖❖❖❖❖❖

When speaking to his disciples about meditation, Joshu, an old master, once said, "If you follow my instruction and do not attain enlightenment, you may cut off my head."

❖❖❖❖❖❖❖

When you meditate, you must have nothing in front and nothing in back. Cancel out your memory of the past; blot out your hope of the future. In that moment there is neither time nor space . . . there is only the eternal present. Zen calls this condition of the mind the "moment of great death," but do not be afraid of this stage in your meditation. Instead of forcing yourself to enter such a condition, just meditate faithfully, either by counting your breath or meditating on your ko-an, and you will be there naturally and gracefully without being aware of the fact. This is the "gateless gate" of Zen. Until you pass this gate, you cannot enter Zen, but when you have passed it, you will realize there was no gate there.

A monk once went to a teacher for personal guidance. The teacher said, "When I clap my hands together, there is a sound. What is the sound of one hand?" The monk worked hard, but could not solve this ko-an. "You are not working hard enough," his teacher told him. "You are attached to food, sleep, name and fame." The next time the monk appeared before his teacher, he fell over as though dead. "You are dead, all right," observed the teacher, "but what about the sound of one hand?" The monk looked up from where he lay on the floor. "I have not solved that as yet." "A dead man tells no story," said the teacher. "Get out, you rascal!" This monk had his teacher before him all the time.

Instead of striving for something to be added to your nature, get rid of all unnecessary opinion, prejudice, pride and the hundred other things that hamper and fetter you. Even your desire for enlightenment will be an obstacle. Just go quietly ahead in your meditation step by step without thought of good or bad, success or failure. "Do not linger where the Buddha is, and where the Buddha is not, pass on quickly."

Nan-in, a master during the Meiji era, received a university professor who came to inquire about Zen.

Nan-in served tea. He poured his visitor's cup full, and then kept on pouring.

The professor watched the overflow until he could no longer restrain himself. "It is overfull. No more will go in!"

"Like this cup," Nan-in replied, "you are full of your own opinions and speculations. How can I show you Zen unless you first empty your cup?"[8]

---

[8] Nyogen Senzaki and Paul Reps. *101 Zen Stories*, David McKay Company, Philadelphia.

SHO-DO-KA

Yoka-daishi (Yung Chia) was an outstanding disciple of Yeno (Hui-neng), the Sixth Patriarch. When he died in 713 A.D., he left a number of works on the Zen approach to enlightenment of which the *Shō-dō-ka* (Song of Realization) is one. The story of Yoka is contained in the *Dan-kyō*, a writing of the Sixth Patriarch, as follows:

Zen Master Gen-kaku of Yoka was born of a Tai family in the state of On-shu. As a youth he studied the Sutras and Shastras,[1] and was well versed in the teaching of Samatha[2] and Vipassana.[3] Through the reading of the *Vimalakirti Nirdesa Sutra,* he realized intuitively the mystery of his own mind, that is, he realized Mind Essence.

A disciple of the Sixth Patriarch by the name of Gen-saku paid him a visit, and during the course of the discussion, noticed that the comments of his friend agreed with the sayings of the various patriarchs. He then asked, "May I know the name of your teacher who transmitted the Dharma to you?"

"I had teachers to instruct me," replied Gen-kaku, "when I studied the Sutras and Shastras of the *Vaipulya* section, but it was through the reading of the *Vimalakirti Nirdesa Sutra* that I realized the significance of the *Buddacitta* (Buddha-heart) School (Dhyana School), and in this respect I have not yet had a teacher to verify and confirm my attainment."

"Before the time of the remote Buddhas," Gen-saku remarked,

[1] Shastras or Sastras: commentaries on the Sutras.
[2] Samatha . . . quietude.
[3] Vipassana . . . contemplation or discernment (Tendai School).

"it was possible to dispense with the service of a teacher, but since that time, he who attains enlightenment without the aid and confirmation of a teacher is a natural heretic."

"Will you kindly act as my testifier?" asked Gen-kaku.

"My words carry no weight," replied his friend. "In So-kei the Sixth Patriarch is to be found to whom visitors in great numbers come from all directions with the common object of having the Dharma transmitted to them. If you wish to go there, I shall be glad to accompany you."

When they reached So-kei to interview the Patriarch, Gen-kaku walked around him three times, then stood still without making obeisance to him.

Noting his discourtesy, the Patriarch said, "A Buddhist monk is the embodiment of three thousand moral precepts and eighty thousand minor disciplinary rules. . . . I wonder where you come from and what makes you so conceited."

"Since the question of incessant re-birth is a momentous one and death may come at any moment, I have no time to waste on ceremony, and wish you to give me a quick answer to this problem."

"Why do you not realize the principle of 'Birthlessness' and thus solve the problem of the transiency of life?" the Patriarch retorted.

"To realize the essence of mind is to be free of re-birth," Gen-kaku replied, "and once this problem is solved, the question of transiency exists no longer."

"That is so. That is so," the Patriarch concurred.

At this moment Gen-kaku made obeisance according to the ceremony of departure.

"You are going away too quickly, are you not?" asked the Patriarch.

"How can there be 'quickness' when motion does not exist intrinsically?" Gen-kaku answered.

"Who knows that motion does not exist?" asked the Patriarch.

"I hope you will not particularize," Gen-kaku observed.

The Patriarch then commended him for his thorough grasp of the idea of "Birthlessness," but Gen-kaku countered, "Is there an idea in 'Birthlessness'?"

"Without an idea, who can particularize?" asked the Patriarch.

"That which particularizes is not an idea," replied Gen-kaku.

"Well said!" exclaimed the Patriarch. He then asked Gen-kaku to delay his departure and spend the night there. From that time on Gen-kaku was known to his contemporaries as the "Enlightened-One-who-had-spent-a-night-with-the-Patriarch."

Sho-do-ka is memorized in its entirety by students in China, Korea, and Japan, and they are often inspired during its recitation.

In *Sho-do-ka* the stanzas have been done directly from a copy of the original into a free translation by Nyogen Senzaki. The commentary, separated from each stanza, is to assist the reader in his understanding and interpretation of the poem, and is Nyogen Senzaki's own instruction to his students.

SHO-DO-KA
by
YOKA-DAISHI

Do you see that Zen student? He has forgotten what he has
  learned, yet he practices easily and freely what he has
  learned and also what he should learn.
He lives in equanimity calmly and contentedly. He is free
  of all care, yet he acts naturally and reasonably.
He neither strives to avoid delusion nor seeks after the truth.
  He knows delusions as baseless and truth as himself.
He sees the true nature of ignorance as Buddha-nature, and
  the true body of his illusionary body as Dharma-kaya,[4]
  the Buddha's eternal body.

Yoka-daishi is admiring and praising the Zen student. He
sees a person who has gone beyond relative good and evil, and
leaves no trace of his learning nor shadow of his doing. He is a
sage who does not look like a sage, and he is a philosopher who
does not carry the odor of philosophy.

If you try to avoid idle thoughts or delusions when you meditate, you cannot enter Samadhi. Whoever seeks after the truth
will remain behind the truth. What you consider idle thoughts
or delusions are nothing but waves on the vast ocean of Buddha-
nature. Just as there are no waves apart from the water, there is
no delusion, no idle thought, no ignorance separate from Buddha-
nature.

[4] Dharma-kaya . . . Law body of the Buddha.

As our bodies are impermanent, it follows that they are empty and visionary. They do not in fact even really belong to us. Your body is not yours, and my body is not mine.

When one realizes completely the Dharma-body,[5] he sees no object.

He, himself, is the source of all things, and his true nature is another name of the eternal Buddha.

Material things and mental phenomena come and go like clouds in the blue sky.

Greed, anger and ignorance . . . these three foams appear and disappear like a mirage on the ocean.

When one recognizes the Dharma-body as such, no matter how beautifully he may define it or describe it, he is still lingering in dualism. But once he has unified himself with the Dharma-body, there is no more and there is no less. He is the Dharma-body, and the Dharma-body is he. He is the source of all things in the universe. His true nature is the eternal Buddha that was never born and will never die.

Greed, anger and ignorance are the three poisons injurious to the good character of man.

A Tibetan Buddhist once wrote: "Greed, anger and ignorance . . . these three stand as obstacles to the way of deliverance; they prevent us in the growth of insight as the roots of the couch-grass prevents the growth of useful plants. If there exist in countries other than Tibet people who have experienced the truth, I cannot say. But I know that among the mighty mountains of my native land there are men and women who can bear witness that in this very life they have attained the supreme goal and tasted

[5] Dharmabody; original man in full; the sound of one hand; the eternal Buddha.

the ultimate deliverance. One must not expect that these enlightened ones will come to live with worldlings, whose most serious actions appear as the play of small children."

This mountaineer does not know Zen at all! Zen students never run away from the three poisons, but see them only as an ephemeral mirage. America has had Zen students in the past, has them in the present, and will have many of them in the future. They mingle easily with so-called worldlings. They play with children; respect kings and beggars; and handle gold and silver as pebbles and stones.

✦✦✦✦✦✦✦

When he realizes the truth, he has no delusion concerning his personal desires nor his self-limited ideas.

He knows that there is no ego entity existing in him, and sees clearly the voidness of all form as merely shadow in relation to both subjective and objective elements.

If you live in this Zen, you can leave hell in your dreams of yesterday, and make your own paradise wherever you stand.

Those without realization, who cheat people with false knowledge, will create a hell during their own lives.

✦✦✦✦✦✦✦

Zen aims at nothing but realization or attainment. Philosophers may postulate reality, driving themselves to the end of the trail of logic, but none of them ever succeeded in attaining. To say that something must be is one thing, but to experience it is another. When Zen asks to hear the sound of one hand, it demands actual experience and nothing else. A student may say that this is the truth, or that this is the absolute. These answers are a ghostly conception, mere shadows of baseless delusions. Why not work deeply enough in meditation to reach the bottom of mind essence? The outcome of this honest, hard work is attainment.

When one attains reality, he actually realizes the truth of all beings. He can prove it by his attitude toward "self-entity" and "self-limited ideas." He knows then that there is no ego entity, that all forms of objectivity are void existing only in terms of relativity. A man may easily free himself of egoism in ethical life, and may even consider himself unselfish in materialistic desire, but if he cannot listen to the opinions of others and insists on conquering the world with his own ideas, he is still the same old egoistic monster.

Zen realization must be manifested in two ways: rejection of an ego substance, and recognition of the voidness of all forms of objectivity. In a ko-an one monk says, "The flag is moving." Another replies, "The wind is moving." The former clings to the entity of the flag. The latter has a broader view, but does not understand true emptiness. The Sixth Patriarch answers them, "The flag is not moving. The wind is not moving. The mind is moving." If you think the Patriarch mentioned mind as a psychological phenomenon, you are entangled in self-limiting ideas.

When Yoka-daishi said, "If you live in this Zen, you can leave hell in your dreams of yesterday, and make your own paradise wherever you stand . . . ," he did not mean that an enlightened man can ignore the law of causation. Man creates his own hell in which to suffer, but who can save him if he does not save himself?

Some religious workers build a brisk business selling people the idea that their sins can be wiped out by another. This was as widely practiced in Yoka-daishi's day as in ours, so he warns such peddlers to beware of what they are creating. Those who speak untruth in this world, bishops or archbishops, reverends or right-reverends, are making a hell here and now.

The minute you attain Buddha's Zen,
The six noble deeds and ten thousand good actions are already complete within you.
In your dream there are six paths,
But when you awake, they will be reduced to nothingness.

Buddha's Zen was transmitted first to Maha-Kasyapa[6] from heart to heart. There is no record in the Sutras about this inner teaching, but one whose meditation is mature receives the same genealogical wisdom. This is the reason why Zen is always living vividly through human experiences, transcending all scriptures and sectarian doctrines. Yoka-daishi called Zen *Tathagata-dhyana*[7] in this work. Later Chinese masters named Zen the *Patriarch's Dhyana*. A name is nothing but a symbol and can never be the thing it stands for. In the future Americans may use a new name for their attainment, otherwise this inner wisdom will never survive in this country. What I say about Zen is my own, nor can it be yours until you reach your own realization.

What are the six noble deeds? They are *Dana* . . . charity; *Sila* . . . keeping the precepts; *Ksanti* . . . perseverance; *Virya* . . . striving; *Dhyana* . . . meditation; *Prajna* . . . wisdom.

What are the six paths? They are *Naraka* . . . hell; *Preta* . . . hungry devil; *Tiryag-yoni* . . . animal mind; *Asura* . . . fighting devil; *Manusya* . . . human being; *Deva* . . . superior man.

Many people recognize these stages as having true existence, but to a Zen student they are nothing but shades of dualistic thought that vanish in the light of realization.

No sin, no happiness, no loss and no gain.
Do not try to seek these things in Mind-Essence.

[6] Maha-Kasyapa . . . a disciple of Buddha and first to receive the Lamp of Dharma, which was later transmitted in a direct line through Bodhi-Dharma, the Patriarchs, etc.
[7] Tathagata-dhyana . . . enlightened meditation.

For a long time you have not wiped the dust from your
    mirror.
Now is the time for you to see its brilliance precisely.

No serious mind can think of sin and bliss in the old way any
more. When a person has experienced realization, it will make
no difference to him whether sins may be blotted out by a supreme being and his agents or some supposed power of hokus-
pokus may give him happiness when he asks for it. These are
idle questions for a Zen student.

In his *Song of Meditation,* Haku-in said: "From the very
beginning you are Buddha. As there is no ice apart from water,
so there is no Buddha outside our fellow beings. Although it is
always within them, people fail to perceive the truth and search
afar for it. They suffer thirst and do not see the fountain near at
hand. They are in poverty and forget that they are heirs to
boundless wealth. You say that you are suffering. You suffer only
because of your own ignorance. Awake from your ignorant
dream! The errors of the past will no longer harass you. Where
is hell? You left it in yesterday's dream. Where is paradise? You
are standing in it."

Your Mind-Essence is bright from the very beginning. This is
the day to see it clearly. This is the moment to begin your work
instantly.

Who thinks non-thinking and who recognizes non-existence?
If it is really non-existence, you cannot think of it.
Ask a robot whether he is happy or not.
As long as you aim to become Buddha,
No matter how you strive, you will never be one.

Do these stanzas seem difficult? Remember that Zen can be
realized but never explained. In your meditation you may already

have experienced "non-thinking." At this moment your "Mind-Mirror" is wiped and polished so thoroughly that there is not even a trace of brilliance remaining. But suppose you hear a dog bark? You visualize a running dog. You think of your pet dog. Then the train of thought passes in front of your nose endlessly. You cannot blame the dog for barking, nor your ears for receiving the sound. But why do you carry it as second thought? If, however, you think you are entering Samadhi, you are already out of it. When you count your breath, just count it. When you meditate on your ko-an, just meditate on it. In meditation you train yourself to carry the one subject of meditation; in daily life do one thing at a time without carrying unnecessary second thought.

Yoka-daishi says, "Ask a robot whether he is happy or not." I can hear you complain, "Is Zen going to compel me to become a robot?" Do you wish to suffer, filling your mind with illusions? Do you know nothing of the joy of giving thoughts enough room in which to stretch themselves and grow? A Zen student has more time to enjoy life because he allows himself to think or to do one thing at a time, and does not block the flow of inner wisdom with the trash of delusions.

"As long as you aim to become Buddha, no matter how you strive, you will never be one." If you cannot find it where you stand, where do you expect to wander in search of it?

> Do not cling to the four elements.
> Drink and eat according to your true nature.
> Things are transient, therefore, they are in a
>   state of emptiness.
> This is Buddha's realization.

Buddhism does not see mind and body as two different things. When it says the four elements, earth, water, fire and wind, it does not mean only the elements of the material world, but also the conditions of the mind as psychological phenomena. In Pali these four elements are called *pathavi* (solidity), *apo* (cohesion), *tejo* (radiability) and *vayu* (movability). Zen does not cling to these elements, but, forgetting both mind and body, lives in Mind-Essence. A Zen student "drinks or eats," that is, lives his everyday life, according to his own true nature.

To illustrate the third and fourth verses of this stanza Tosotsu's ko-an, from the *Gateless Gate,* will be used. "First, in studying Zen the aim is to see one's own true nature. Now where is your true nature? Second, when one realizes his own true nature, he will be free from birth and death. Now, when you shut the light from your eyes, and become a corpse, how can you free yourself? Third, if you free yourself from birth and death, you should know where you are. Now, your body separates into four elements, where are you?"

Do not think of good with your mind and body. Do not think of bad with your mind and body. Forget that you have a mind and body. Make your present minute the only true life you have. If an idea disturbs you, think of the impermanency of worldly things. When the illusions of individual entity vanish, the gate of true meditation will be opened. With empty hands and with empty mind you can meet your true self there. Who said that there is Buddha's realization? Do not be cheated by Yoka-daishi or anyone else. Just find it out for yourself.

A true disciple of Buddha speaks the ultimate truth.
If you do not agree with what I say, you are free to discuss it.
You must remember, however, that Buddhism is concerned
    with the root of truth,
Not with the branches or leaves.

What is the ultimate truth? Yoka-daishi says that all things are transient and ultimately empty, and once this is seen there is realization. Southern Buddhists express the ultimate truth with three Pali words . . . *anicca, dukkha,* and *anatta. Anicca* expresses impermanence, your mind, your body and the world you live in. One does not realize this fact, and so clings to what he likes. When he cannot hold it, he suffers, and this is known as *dukkha.* Life is an eternal flow. If you cannot hold even the mind and body you use, how can you expect to cling to other things and hold them? "Not I" is represented by *anatta.* When you understand these three characteristics, you will come to the real "I" . . . your true self.

Northern Buddhists express these fundamentals of Buddhism by 1) admitting the impermanence of all things; 2) denying absolutely the existence of individual soul; 3) aiming at ultimate reality (Nirvana).[8]

When Yoka-daishi said, "If you do not agree with what I say, you are free to discuss it," he was not inviting argument for the sake of debate. You cannot convince others of Zen through argument. No matter how cleverly logical you may be in cornering your opponent, you cannot give him enlightenment unless he opens his own eyes to attain it. You may clear his doubts by reasoning, but he must reach the root by himself.

Most people do not recognize the mani-jewel,
    the gem of wisdom.
It is hidden in the secret place of Tathagata
    awaiting discovery and attainment.
The six senses and the six worlds interweave
    making life as it is.

[8] Nirvana . . . synonymous with enlightenment, but is not a negative condition as many suppose, nor a condition of non-existence, nor is it to be sought outside of *Samsara,* the world of birth and death.

It is an illusion as a whole, yet nothing exists
to be called illusion.
The perfect light of this mani-jewel, the gem
of wisdom, illuminates humanity.
It has neither color nor form, nor has it non-
color and non-form.

❖❖❖❖❖❖❖

The mani-jewel is a legendary gem of old India that fulfills all desires of its possessor. Buddhists work for desirelessness, treasuring calmness and contentment and looking forward to the highest wisdom and moral perfection. Yoka-daishi uses "mani-jewel" metaphorically saying that it can be found in "the secret place of the Tathagata." But Tathagata has nothing to do with time or place.

Your eyes create the world of color and form; your ears, the world of sound; your nose, the world of odor; your tongue the world of sapidity; and your brain, the world of thought. The six-fold function is manifested as numerous images of the moon may appear on ponds, lakes or the sea, or as many waves may rise and fall on the selfsame body of the great ocean.

Everything just appears through contact of subjective and objective elements, and you simply recognize and name them in terms of relativity. This is the performance of the mani-jewel, which, subjectively, you call your true self, and objectively, Buddha nature.

❖❖❖❖❖❖❖

Clarify the five kinds of vision, and acquire
the five powers.
It is possible only through Zen meditation
that goes beyond speculation.
One can see the images in the mirror naturally.
To hold the reflection of the moon on the
water is impossible.

❖❖❖❖❖❖❖

The five kinds of vision are the physical, heavenly, prajna, dharma and Buddha vision. The five powers are faith, energy, memory, meditation and wisdom. One attains these five types of vision and power through unification with Mind-Essence, where they are facets of the same gem of wisdom.

Everyone knows that the physical eye must have light in order to see, and that even then it is not to be relied upon implicitly.

Modern science has developed the heavenly eye in the telescope and the microscope, bringing into the range of vision things that could not otherwise be seen.

The prajna or wisdom eye views the world without desire, and the person who possesses it can avoid entangling, dualistic thoughts.

The dharma eye is the eye of higher wisdom in the world of discrimination. A Zen student who has sound knowledge of modern science and philosophy, is well acquainted with other religions and the cultures of many lands so that he may view the condition of other beings with sympathy and tolerance, is one using the vision of dharma.

The Buddha eye is the perfect eye. When a student has attained complete realization, he sees the world in truth as it is in reality. This is the eye of perfect compassion free of all defilement.

The five powers are self-evident. Faith allows one to stand firmly in truth; energy is necessary to continue the climb; memory increases and enriches knowledge; meditation guards a person's calmness, which is the source of the fifth power, prajna, the wisdom of emancipation.

Yoka-daishi often speaks of the "mirror." This mirror belongs to each one of us, ready to use. It is easy to recognize the images it seems to contain, but the moment you think you have them, they have vanished. "Who can hold the reflection of the moon on the water?"

The five kinds of vision are inherent in Zen realization, and the five powers manifest as you practice Zen in your everyday life. The secret is to live every minute in Zen. Receive, use, then forget what you saw in your mirror, knowing they are only reflections with no self-entity.

A Zen student should walk alone at all times.
Those who have attained, tread the same road
of Nirvana.
Each of them is natural in manner, and clean
and contented of heart.
Since not one of them is concerned with special attraction, no one pays him special
attention.

In the Old Testament, Psalms 10:1, David complains, "Why standest thou afar off, O Lord? Why hidest thou thyself in times of trouble?" No matter how closely God approaches David, they are still two and not one. A Zen student worships no god, observes no orthodox rites, does not look forward to a future abode, nor has a soul to be cared for by anyone else. He walks freely, unburdened by dogmatic, theological postulation, knowing that as he masters his situation, wherever he stands is the land of truth. His Zen training and meditation are for nothing but his perfect emancipation.

He walks alone in Mind-Essence. Who calls it the road of Nirvana? He has no such road ahead of him. He goes ahead step by step naturally and wisely. His heart is clean and he is always contented. He works hard, therefore, he is strong. He is not worried about his appearance, and so attracts no attention. He lives among men quietly and easily.

The followers of Buddha speak of their poverty.
The simplicity of their living may be called poor,
    but not their Zen.
A monk's gown, torn and mended, shows the
    world his poverty;
His Zen, unseen by others, is the treasure beyond
    all value.

A Chinese Zen master was once asked to name the most valuable treasure in the world. He answered that it was the head of a dead cat. When questioned as to his reason for this answer, he replied, "Because no one can name the price." How would you like to become the head of a dead cat? Zen students! Philosophers! Occult students! Metaphysicians! Theologians! Atheists! They are all noisy, living cats with their price clearly written on their foreheads! A true seeker of enlightenment cannot display his value.

No matter how much it is used, the priceless treasure never
    deteriorates.
It may be given freely to others who need it.
The three bodies of Buddha and the four kinds of wisdom
    are completely contained in it.
The eight sorts of emancipation and the six miraculous
    powers are merely impressions of the same seal.

Taku-an, a Japanese Zen master, wrote a poem of eight Chinese characters which reads:

> Not twice this day
> Inch time foot gem.

In a free translation to the English these words mean:

This day will not come again.
Each minute is worth a priceless gem.

The three bodies of Buddha are considered to be the Dharma-body, the Attainment body, and the Transformation body. Each one of us has the Dharma body; through realization it becomes the body of Attainment; and in our daily action and associations with others it produces the Transformation body.

The four kinds of wisdom are the mirror intuition, the intuition of identity, the clear perception of relations, and the knowledge of work.

The eight-fold emancipation is emancipation by materialism; emancipation by idealism; emancipation by aestheticism; emancipation by relativity; emancipation by spiritualism; emancipation by Hinayana thought; emancipation by distinction of Hinayana and Mahayana teaching; emancipation by prajnaparamita, the understanding of emptiness in Mahayana teaching.

The six miraculous powers are geographical, visual, auditory, fatal, psychic and purification.

There is no need to memorize these lists. Everything is contained in your realization. When you attain enlightenment, you are like a person who possesses a seal. You may make many impressions on varying materials, the color and the shade may also vary, but each is made by the one seal of ultimate wisdom.

The priceless treasure belongs to everyone. Each of us is a part of Dharmakaya, but how can we realize it until we meditate and obtain the fruit of our striving? This is the body of attainment, but attainment does not denote static conclusion. It is the pure force used to serve humanity, which service is called the body of transformation. When you hear the sound of one hand, you have mirror-intuition. When you can put out a light one thousand miles away, you are practicing your intuition of identity. When you can tell me whether the man you meet is your younger brother or older brother, you have a clear perception of relations. When you can show me how you enter an object, such as a stick of incense, and pay homage to all the Buddhas, you are proving your knowledge of doing work in Zen. As for emancipation, what a foolish idea to make it eightfold! The blue skies have no limit! We merely designate the floating clouds as being here or there.

Your geographical miracle is accomplished when you bring me some snow from the top of Mt. Whitney; your auditory miracle when you hear the song of angels in the thirty-third heaven; your fatal miracle when you know where you were when Gautama Buddha was born in India; your psychic miracle when you know the one whose servants are the present Buddha, past Buddhas, and future Buddhas; and your miracle of purification when you avoid all evil thoughts and actions to develop good thoughts and right actions, not only for yourself but for all with whom you associate. Miracles! What nonsense! Just use each moment of the law of causation.

The excellent student of Zen goes directly to the
    ultimate truth.
The fair or good ones like to learn from others but
    have no steady faith.
Once you strip off the tattered clothing of preju-
    dice you will see your true self.
How can you wander around in outward striving?

Mu-so Kokushi, a Japanese Zen master, once spoke of the three types of students. First, there were those who threw off all entangling conditions to apply themselves wholeheartedly to the study of Zen; second, there came those who were not so single-minded seeking a solution in books or other activities; the third and lowest group was made up of students who mouthed the words of Buddha or the Patriarchs instead of digging for the treasure within themselves.

If Zen is not a teaching which can settle the matter once and for all, then a lay student has little chance of becoming a first class disciple. Zen belongs to the abrupt school of Buddhism. You may spend a long time mining for your inner treasure, but the moment you unearth it, you will see its brilliance instantly. Those who insist that you will find only a fragment at a time are like those who would carry out the darkness before lighting a room.

You can forget your worries of the past and future to live only in the peaceful present. Each moment contains an opportunity for you to be an excellent student of Zen.

❖❖❖❖❖❖❖

> Some may slander or argue against Zen.
> They are playing with fire, trying to burn the
>   heavens in vain.
> A true student of Zen will take their words
>   as sweet dew-drops,
> Forgetting even this sweetness when he
>   enters the region of non-thinking.

❖❖❖❖❖❖❖

A Zen student will find few people who agree with his beliefs, nor understand his effortless effort. Other sects of Buddhism decree that a student must go through many stages even to hope to attain enlightenment in a future incarnation, and other religions will find many points of difference on which to hang their arguments. Since argument never convinced anyone, let alone enlightened him, a Zen student will avoid all fruitless discussion, helping others whenever he can without seeking assistance for himself. He knows where his treasure lies and how to use it.

One night many years ago a blind man, visiting a friend, was offered a lantern to carry home with him. "I do not need a lantern," he said, "darkness and light are the same to me." "I know you do not need a lantern to find your way home," his friend replied, "but if you do not take it, someone else may run into you. You must take it." The blind man took the lantern, but before he had gone very far, someone walked straight into him. "Look where you're going," the blind man exclaimed. "Can't you see this lantern?" "Your candle has burned out," the stranger answered.

Always be sure your candle is burning, both for your own safety and for the sake of others.

I observe abusive words as virtuous action,
And consider the abuser as one of my good teachers.
Since my feeling is neither for nor against the abuser,
Why should I express the two powers of perseverance,
    the knowledge of the unborn and the love of all
    beings?

In the preceding stanza Yoka-daishi teaches the negative attitude towards slanderers, whereas this one regards the abuser positively. A man may confess his sins to God, but does not care to have another person criticize one of his minor faults. Much as he may admit deserving such criticism, it is painful to him. A Zen student not only listens, but accepts the words with gratitude.

When Yoka-daishi asks, "Why should I express the two powers of perseverance," he means to avoid fussing about "reasons," worrying about "why" and "because." When there is no cognition of "I" or "he," there is no relativity of "I" and "not I." This is the knowledge of the unborn. Every Bodhissatva or Zen student loves all sentient beings irrespective of appearance or condition. He does not fall into the trap of dualism, saying, "This man has slandered me. I shall be especially loving to him." His knowledge and love are expressed in all he thinks and does as naturally as the sun shines upon the earth or a white cloud floats across the blue sky.

> One who attains Zen must acquire its eloquence.
> Meditation and wisdom must have their full bril-
>   liance unclouded by an idea of emptiness.
> Such an accomplishment is not limited to the few.
> The Buddhas, countless as the sands of the Ganges,
>   are all witness to this fact.

There are four kinds of eloquence. First, the eloquence of Dhamma permits you to express the ultimate wisdom once you attain enlightenment. A single act may adequately express your interpretation of inner wisdom when you gain realization. Second is the eloquence of reason. Buddhism is a religion of reason. If your eyes are clear, you should have no difficulty in reporting what you see. Third is the eloquence of utterance. Zen students should use their words economically. People waste words because they lack concentration. If silence is golden, it would seem that there are entirely too many silver pieces in circulation these days. Fourth is the eloquence of compassion. When you have learned to lead a pure, unselfish life, your words will become kind and powerful.

Beginners in meditation often cling one-sidedly to an erroneous idea of emptiness, refusing positive action or remaining coldly distant from the world. Once they have experienced true empti-ness, however, their love is greater than that of even the kindest unenlightened person.

This accomplishment is not limited to a few people, as the innumerable Buddhas (enlightened ones) will bear witness.

> The fearless thought of Zen is like the
>   mighty roar of the lion,
> Striking terror in the hearts of other beasts.
> Even the king of elephants will run away
>   forgetting his pride.
> Courageous students alone, like the dragon,
>   hear the roar with calm pleasure.

When a Zen student comes for San-zen,[9] he strikes the bell twice without the slightest fear. In that moment he transcends both birth and death; he is beyond space and time. What he says now comes directly from his own Buddha nature, and is called the "roar of the lion." This does not mean that he shouts. He is not an empty radio turned on at full volume. His speech is the result of his own hard work, and even though I reject his answer, his calmness is unbroken. Sometimes a student will bring a bag full of answers, trying one after another to fit the question, but he is like a pedlar in a vain attempt to please a customer. Instead of reaching the palace of wisdom, he will return to his old alley of blind faith with all the stray cats that symbolize superstition.

In Asia it is said that, "To study Zen requires the spirit of a hero." Zen will never appeal to the masses. In all ages students of Zen have been intelligent, compassionate and courageous, then, when they attain realization, they help each person according to his need. They are not quacks prescribing one panacea for all ailments, but wise physicians assisting each person to cure his

[9] San-zen . . . from Chinese *San-Ch'an*, to study Zen, especially the examination of a student by a teacher.

particular illness. They have accomplished their meditation, and their one aim is to aid all sentient beings to achieve the same.

❖❖❖❖❖❖❖❖

> Zen students journey by land and sea, across
>   rivers and over mountains,
> Visiting monasteries and receiving personal
>   guidance from teachers.
> I also followed the way, reaching So-kei, where
>   I met my master and received Dhamma.
> Now I know my true being has nothing to
>   do with birth and death.

❖❖❖❖❖❖❖❖

It took Yoka-daishi many years to reach So-kei. He had to cross the rivers of speculation, the sea of intellectuality, where many contemporary scholars had drifted off their course never to reach the shores of Nirvana, and finally he had to climb the mountains of meditation to attain self-realization. The Sixth Patriarch did not bestow Dhamma on Yoka, he only affirmed the latter's attainment.

Although many of the ko-ans and Zen stories are woven around traveling or secluded monks, nothing will be achieved by our clinging to and imitating these outward circumstances. A Zen student is neither a misanthropist nor a misogynist, so there is no point in shutting himself up in some forest cabin or avoiding the opposite sex. He must control his own environment and master his situation wherever he stands.

In order to know the author of this poem intimately, we must remember the last line of the stanza, "Now I know my true being has nothing to do with birth and death." This is your ko-an. How can you free yourself from birth and death? What is your true being? No, no! Do not think about it! Just gaze at it closely.

A Zen student walks in Zen and sits in Zen.
Whether in speech and action, or silence and in-
    action, his body always dwells in peace.
He smiles, facing the sword that takes his life.
He keeps his poise even at the moment of death,
    nor can drugs alter his calm.

Meditation is practiced in four ways. First, your mind and
body are still. This is the source of all your Zen actions. Second,
your body is still but your mind moves, as in reading or listening
to a lecture. Third, your mind is still but your body moves, as in
walking. Fourth, your mind and body move as you do your work
in daily life. Thus at each moment a good Zen student experiences the Mind-Essence ever at ease.

Our great teacher, Sakyamuni, met Dipankara Buddha[10]
    many millions of years ago, and accepted his Dhamma.
Ever since, he is master of Ksanti, perseverance, life after
    life.

Some people may be interested in past lives, but Zen students
see life as eternal presence. Stories of "incarnation" insinuate
the idea of individual personality distorting the vision of truth
seekers. When you extend time and narrow space, you will see
Buddha Sakyamuni receiving Dhamma from Dipankara Buddha
many millions of years ago, but when you extend space and
flatten time, you will see Ksanti, perseverance, mastering human
affairs. It is the actual business of the present moment. Until
students of occultism understand this and come to their senses,
spiritual gold-diggers will strike it rich here and abroad.

[10] Dipankara Buddha . . . one of the early Buddhas before the time of Gautama Buddha.

Man is born many times, so he dies many times.
Life and death continue endlessly.
If he realizes the true meaning of unborn,
He will transcend both gladness and grief.

❖❖❖❖❖❖❖❖

He lives alone in a mountain hut
Among the old pine trees,
Meditating comfortably
And living peacefully.

❖❖❖❖❖❖❖❖

Those who understand Dhamma always act
    naturally.
Most people in the world live in samskrita,[11] but
    Zen students live in asamskrita.[12]
Those who give something to others to receive
    something in return,
Are shooting arrows heavenwards.

❖❖❖❖❖❖❖❖

The arrow, which was shot against heaven, returns
    to the earth.
When striving and gaining are balanced, nothing
    remains.
Aimless striving is quite different,
It opens the gate of truth leading to the garden of
    Tathagata.
A true Zen student ignores the branches and leaves
    until he reaches the root.
It is like the image of the moon reflected in the
    water of a jade bowl.
The real beauty of the mani-gem, treasure of
    emancipation, I now know, . . .
I and others are benefited eternally.

[11] Samskrita . . . subject to causation, the world of birth and death.
[12] Asamskrita . . . not subject to causation, the world of birthlessness and deathlessness.

We devote ourselves to meditation in order to reach the root of the teaching. Do not ask me any foolish questions. First of all find out who you really are. The reflection of the moon on the water is beautiful, but the moon itself is not there nor is its beauty lingering in the sky.

> The moon rises above the river, the wind plays
>   softly in the pines on the shore
> All night long. What is the meaning of this
>   serenity?
> You must see the precepts of Buddha-nature vividly
>   imprinted.
> Dew, fog, cloud and mist clothe the original man
>   in full.

This stanza is a ko-an. You must work hard to catch a glimpse of it. If you think that I am hiding something from you, you are the guilty one. I am concealing nothing from you.

> A begging bowl once conquered dragons and a staff
>   pacified fighting tigers.
> The staff had six rings on top whose tinkling called
>   people from their dreams.
> The bowl and the staff are not mere symbols of the
>   teaching,
> But Tathagata's actual work remaining in the world.

Legend says that Buddha Sakyamuni conquered dragons making them so small that they stayed in his begging bowl. With his staff a Zen master once stopped the fighting of two tigers and so saved them from killing each other. These stories are neither symbols nor miracles. When you attain the mani-gem, you can perform the same deeds.

Where are the burdens of egoism you have carried many years? Where are the dualistic ideas that fight continuously in your mind? Look! The moon rises above the river of Samsara.[13] The wind plays the melody of Buddha-Dhamma in the pines on the shore. What is the meaning of this serenity? Now you have no burden of egoism nor discord of dualism. Is this a miracle? Anyone can experience it if he has the courage to break his delusions and face himself as he has always been beyond time and space.

❖❖❖❖❖❖❖

An ideal Zen student neither seeks the true nor
    avoids the untrue.
He knows that these are merely dualistic ideas that
    have no form.
Non-form is neither empty nor not empty.
It is the true form of Buddha's wisdom.

❖❖❖❖❖❖❖

To assist you in the interpretation of this last stanza I shall paraphrase a portion of *Shin-jin-mei,* a poem written by the Third Patriarch in China. "Truth is like vast space without entrance or exit. There is nothing more nor nothing less. Foolish people limit themselves, covering their eyes, but truth is never hidden. Some attend lectures trying to grasp truth in the words of others. Some accumulate books trying to dig truth from the pile of trash. They are both wrong. A few of the wiser ones may learn meditation in their effort to reach an inner void. They chose the void rather than outer entanglements, but it is still the same old dualistic trick. Just think non-thinking if you are a true

[13] Samsara . . . the world of birth and death.

Zen student. There you do not know anything, but you are with everything. There is no choice nor preference and dualism will vanish by itself. But if you stop moving and hold quietness, that quietness is ever in motion. If children make a noise, you will scold them loudly so that the situation is worse than before. Just forget and ignore the noise, and you will attain peace of mind. When you forget your liking and disliking, you will get a glimpse of oneness. The serenity of this middle way is quite different from the inner void."

❖❖❖❖❖❖❖

The mind mirror illumines all ingenuously.
Its penetrating, limitless rays reach everywhere in
    the universe.
Without exception everything is reflected in this
    mirror.
The whole universe is a gem of light beyond the
    terms of in and out.

❖❖❖❖❖❖❖

Here is another portion of *Shin-jin-mei* to interpret the preceding stanza: "Zen transcends time and space. Ten thousand years are nothing but a thought after all. What you have seen is what you had in the whole world. If your thought transcends time and space, you will know that the smallest thing is large and the largest thing is small, that being is non-being and non-being is being. Without such experience you will hesitate to do anything. If you can realize that one is many, and many are one, your Zen will be completed.

"Faith and mind-essence are not separate from each other. You will see only the 'not two.' The 'not two' is the faith. The 'not two' is the mind-essence. There is no other way but silence to express it properly. This silence is not the past. This silence is not the present. This silence is not the future."

When a Zen-student sees emptiness onesidedly, he
　　is likely to ignore the law of causation.
He will then live aimlessly with evil thoughts and
　　wrong actions.
His idea is morbid as he denies the existence of
　　anything, but admits an entity of emptiness.
To escape drowning he has thrown himself into
　　the fire.

To "see emptiness onesidedly" is to give another name to relativity, phenomenality or nothingness. When Buddhism denies
the existence of anything, this of course includes the existence of
emptiness. There is order, there is the law of causation. The use
of the word "emptiness" implies that which cannot be spoken.

He who rejects delusions to search for truth,
May achieve skill in discrimination,
But such a student will never reach enlightenment
Because he mistakes his enemy for his own dear child.

Some Christians admire an angel but hate a devil. Some Con-
fucians pine for the ancient kingdom but complain of the present
government. All of them attempt to take hold of the true by
abandoning the false. They struggle endlessly, but never attain
true peacefulness. Zen students who try to reach truth by reject-
ing delusions are making the same mistake. Scientists reduce
matter to atoms, then divide the atom as they divided the mole-
cule. They are driven to the dilemma that matter is infinitely
divisible, which is inconceivable, or that there is a limit to its
divisibility, which is also inconceivable. It is the same with time
and space. When we analyze matter, we find nothing at last but

force; a force impressed upon our organs of sense, or a force resisting our organs of action. Who shall tell us what force is? When we turn from physics to psychology, we come upon mind and consciousness. Here are greater puzzles than before.

We must not postulate the true outside the untrue. We must see holiness transmuting unholy conditions. We must establish the kingdom of heaven here and now. The terms given by science and philosophy are based upon dualistic delusions, no matter what skill there is in discrimination. Do not become enchanted by such expressions as "God within," or "I am That," but experience the Samadhi where there is no god, within or without, where there is no this, no that, no I and no you. Then you may use the Christian terms freely, if you like, and say, "God not in the world is a false God, and the world not in God is unreality." Until that time, learn silence and work on constantly in silence, to see clearly what the mind is.

❖❖❖❖❖❖❖

> Man misses the spiritual treasure and loses the
>   proper merit
> Because he depends on dualistic thinking and
>   neglects the essence of mind.
> To pass through the gate of Zen one must correct
>   this error.
> Then he can attain the wisdom to enter the palace
>   of Nirvana.

❖❖❖❖❖❖❖

Buddhists often refer to the "seven treasures," which are faith, perseverance, listening, humility, precepts, self-surrender, and meditation and wisdom. (Meditation and wisdom are considered as one—inner cultivation and outer illumination.) To acquire these seven treasures one must first of all see his own Mind-Essence clearly, just as Aladdin had first to find the lamp before he could produce other wonders.

Wobaku, a Chinese Zen master, once said, "Buddhas and sentient beings both grow out of One Mind, and there is no reality other than this Mind. . . . Only because we seek it outwardly in a world of form, the more we seek the farther away it moves from us. To make Buddha seek after himself, or to make Mind take hold of itself . . . this is impossible to the end of eternity. We do not realize that as soon as our thoughts cease and all attempts at forming ideas are forgotten, the Buddha is revealed before us."

The true student of Zen carries the sword of Prajna (the wisdom of emancipation),
The blade is so sharp that one feels the searing flame around it.
It cuts away the delusions of non-Buddhist thought as well as the haughty pride of heavenly devils.

Sometimes the student preaches like a thunder storm;
Sometimes, he pours the gentle rain of loving kindness.
He walks like the king of the elephants, yet always loves other beings.
He teaches five students of different nature, leading them to Buddhahood, although they come to him through the three different gates.

"Heavenly devils" are those who call themselves Zen masters or those who wear the robes of various religious sects, and think that by so doing they have been equally invested with some divine right to direct the lives of others. Pride is one of the most subtle and insidious evils of all, appearing in many forms. Only the student who has accomplished Prajna has any right to lead others.

The five types of students are those who enter Buddhahood

by realizing the four noble truths (Çravaka), the twelve nida-nas[14] (Pratyeka-buddha), or the six paramitas (Bodhisattva), some students are uncertain, and others fit none of these categories. Even so, the true student of Zen guides each according to his understanding until he attains enlightenment.

❖❖❖❖❖❖❖

The precious grass of the Himalayas is the only
    kind in the meadow.
Cows that graze there give the best milk from
    which is made the richest cheese.
Zen students partake of teaching always as pure.
When human character is purified, it is the char-
    acter of all beings;
When the law of humanity is completed, it is the
    law of the universe.
One moon is reflected on many waters;
Innumerable reflections are nothing but the image
    of one moon.
The Dharma-kaya of all Buddhas becomes my
    inner being;
My inner being is unified with Tathagata.
One stage of meditation contains all other stages
    completely;
The Essence of Mind is not limited by color, form,
    thought nor any activity.
A snap of the fingers and eight thousand gates of
    the teaching are established.
A wink of the eye and countless ages of time have
    vanished.
Innumerable names and categories have nothing
    to do with my realization.

❖❖❖❖❖❖❖

"One touch of nature makes the whole world kin." All things return to one, and one operates in all things. When you pass one

14 Nidana . . . the process of Karma relation.

ko-an, you have passed all ko-ans. It is your own fault if you are entangled by the next one. Realization has no color, no form, no psychological movement, and no action of dualistic tendency.

> You cannot praise nor blame realization.
> Like the sky truth has no bounds.
> Wherever you stand, it surrounds you.
> When you seek it, you cannot reach it;
> Your hand cannot hold it, nor your mind exclude it.
> When you no longer seek it, it is with you.
> In silence, you speak it loudly; in speech you
>   manifest its silence.
> Thus the gate of compassion opens wide to the
>   benefit of all beings.

When you begin to study Zen, you aim to attain realization. Your motive is good in so far as motive is concerned, but in your meditation you should aim at nothing. You may aim at realization to encourage yourself when you are not meditating, but beware of clinging entanglements. Encouragement is one thing, meditation is another. Do not mix them up. Carry your meditation as the eternal present, and saturate your everyday life in it.

> When a person asks me what branch of Buddhism
>   I studied,
> I tell him about Mahaprajna, the root of the
>   teaching.
> Without Mahaprajna, though you know right and
>   wrong, you are beyond the truth.
> With the root of the teaching, wherever you go is
>   the land of truth.
> I studied Mahaprajna for many, many lives;

This statement is neither to deceive you nor trick
you.
I was told to spread the teaching;
The order came from Buddha through the genera-
tions.
The lamp of wisdom was first transmitted to
Mahakasyapa,
Then genealogically through twenty-eight Patri-
archs.
Bodhidharma, the last Patriarch of India, came
to this country across the seas.
My teacher, who works in So-kei, received his robe
To become the Sixth Patriarch in this land, as
you have heard.
Who knows how many generations will carry the
teaching in the future?

Buddhism is the teaching of self-enlightenment. No God or
gods will help you to realize the truth. The power of realization
within you is called Mahaprajna, meaning great wisdom. This is
the root of the teaching, the source of all streams of Buddhistic
thought. Those who speculate, reading scriptures or clinging to
creeds and dogmas, wander far from realization. Ethical deeds
and kind actions may be praised, but they are without real value
until they spring from Mahaprajna.

When Yoka speaks of having studied for many, many lives, he
is not referring to innumerable incarnations. When he attained
his Zen, he lost his selfish delusions to become one with the
vast ocean of wisdom whose waves of Buddhas and Patriarchs
were also his. The brilliancy of Mahaprajna illumines all beings;
Buddhas and Patriarchs reflect this brilliance one to the other.

Yoka gives a brief history of Zen, then wonders how future
generations will carry the teaching. To discover or to ignore the
latent Mahaprajna is the individual choice of each person.

The true does not stand by itself, and the false
never exists alone.
When the idea of existence and non-existence van-
ishes, the idea of emptiness and non-emptiness
disappears.
The Sutra gives twenty names to emptiness, each
showing you the one body of Buddha-nature.
The mind rises and contacts the outer world, thus
delusions appear.
Subjectivity and objectivity are like dust on the
surface of a mirror.
When the mirror is free of dust, it shines brightly.
If no mind rises, there is no contact, no delusion
. . . only the true nature of man appears.

❖❖❖❖❖❖❖

Yoka is warning us not to postulate true and false. Without
dualism man can easily reach the truth, but he must experience
it in his meditation. The goal of meditation is beyond words and
ideas. The names of emptiness are like the lists of drugs. If you
are well and strong, you are not interested in them. Many
teachers seek to hold or to mystify a student by using the various
designations of good or evil built up through the ages. If you
wish to make a business of teaching, then memorize the names,
but if you want emancipation for yourself and others, give up the
drug business and practice Zen meditation.

❖❖❖❖❖❖❖

It is sad to live in the time when Dhamma is not
practiced and evil thoughts grow.
The people cannot accept true teaching and cannot
discipline themselves.
They live far from wisdom, clinging to wrong
ideas.
Evil is strong and disciples are weak, fear and
hatred are spreading.

Even though they hear of the intuitive teaching of
  Tathagata,
They desire to crush it under their heels.

❖❖❖❖❖❖❖

There are three processes of Buddhism to establish the teaching in contemporary minds: first, the teaching must be well
understood; second, it must be strictly practiced; third, it must
be precisely realized and actualized.

This stanza refers to the Sutra in which Buddha said that one
thousand years after his death the people would learn Dhamma,
practice it and attain its fruits; for the next thousand years people
will learn the teaching, and some may practice it, but will not
continue until they attain its fruits; for the next ten thousand
years people may hear about Dhamma, but they will not practice
it, so of course they will not attain enlightenment. A person
chooses his own era . . . accuracy, imitation, or degeneration. He
may study for years only to accumulate knowledge (his age of
degeneration), but if he is brave and sincere enough to concentrate his study of meditation, next week may be his era of
imitation or accuracy.

❖❖❖❖❖❖❖

Craving produces action effecting man's suffering.
It is useless to blame others when you reap what
  you have sown.
Those who do not wish to suffer in hell,
Should not slander the Wheel of Dhamma.

❖❖❖❖❖❖❖

When Buddha taught the law of causation to his disciples, he
said, "Actions are determined by ignorance; by action consciousness is determined; by consciousness are determined name and

shape; by name and shape the senses are determined; the senses determine contact; by contact feeling is determined; by feeling craving is determined; by craving grasping is determined; grasping determines becoming; by becoming birth is determined; by birth are age and death determined, sorrow, grief, woe, lamentation and despair. Such is the arising of all this mass of ill."

Any Zen teacher will warn you that there is no equality without discrimination, and that there is no discrimination without equality, but few students understand the nuance of meaning.

It is a self-evident fact that each person, irrespective of attainment, is subject to the law of causation. If he would terminate his own suffering and help others as well, let him work in accord with the law of the universe rather than strive to evade it.

❖❖❖❖❖❖❖

No other trees grow in the forest of Chandana[15]
    wood;
For countless ages only lions have lived there,
Roaming freely in the silent, dark grove.
No birds and no other animals enter the forest,
Only the lion cubs follow the older beasts. . . .
Even the three-year-old roars loudly.
How can a yelping fox imitate the king of Dhamma?
Even though hundreds of monsters open their
    mouths, it will be in vain.

❖❖❖❖❖❖❖

It is said in India that no inferior trees grow near a forest of Chandana, so Buddhists use the name as a symbol of ultimate wisdom. In this stanza birds and beasts represent fame and glory. Monks are indifferent to these in any form in any age. Only the lion cubs can follow the older lions, and even they have learned to roar while still young. A yelping fox may fool some with his

15 Chandana . . . sandal wood.

imitations, as a false teacher will use the words and rituals of true teachings, but when he meets a real lion he will be helpless.

> Zen doctrine is no subject for sentiment.
> Doubts cannot be cleared by argument.
> I stubbornly demand your silence
> To save you from the pitfall of being and
>   non-being.

Zen allows no student to waste his time even for a second. If you have a ko-an, work on it; if you have no ko-an, just count your breath. Doubt? What is it? Just keep on meditating. This is the only means of learning to walk the Middle Way.

> Wrong is not always wrong, nor right always right.
> If you cling to fixed ideas, a tenth of an inch's differ-
>   ence will set you ten thousand miles away.
> When she reaches the source, the infant female dragon
>   enters Buddhahood;
> When he fails to touch the essence, a learned disciple
>   of Buddha suffers the tortures of hell.

The *Saddharma-pundarika-sutra* mentions an infant female dragon that attained realization, and in the *Mahaparinirvana-sutra* is found the story of Zen-sho, the learned disciple, who suffered the tortures of hell. But why search the scriptures when we witness such examples every day of our lives? Sex, age or intellectuality have nothing to do with enlightenment.

From early youth I have accumulated the know-
ledge of Buddhism, studying the Sutras and
Sastras.
I had no time to rest as I classified the terms of the
teaching.
Like a man counting the grains of sand on the
shore, I tired myself in vain.
I felt that Buddha scolded me as I read his words
in the Sutra,
"Why name the price of your neighbor's treasure?"
For years I travelled in the wrong direction,
Like a prodigal son wandering from his home.

◆◆◆◆◆◆◆

A Zen student must spend more time in meditation than he
does in reading . . . even Zen books. Without your own experience you will be a stranger to Zen and a philosophical tramp.
Find your own treasure.

◆◆◆◆◆◆◆

A man whose character is wrongly developed seldom understands things correctly.
It is difficult for him to attain the abrupt wisdom
of Tathagata.
Two classes of students seek emancipation for
themselves, not for the love of sentient beings.
Worldly scholars have dualistic knowledge, but
they lack Prajna, the wisdom of emancipation.

◆◆◆◆◆◆◆

Confucius said, "By nature men are almost alike; by practice
they are far apart." Those who love all sentient beings will meditate to save them, thereby developing their own character in
Zen. The mind of Çravaka is ready to listen to an enlightened
man, but only to eliminate its own suffering. Some study Zen to

overcome weakness such as temper, cowardliness and excitability. These are selfish students. The mind of Pratyeka-Buddha is also alert for study, but its motive is not altruistic. Non-Buddhistic scholars have dualistic knowledge, which makes them intellectual, but they lack Prajna and realize that their efforts will not bring mankind true happiness.

❖❖❖❖❖❖❖

Those who are stupid and childish wander beyond realization.
When they see a closed fist, they assume there is something in it.
If you point your finger to the moon, they discuss the finger, not the moon.
Their thought never goes beyond the five senses as they play hide and seek in the material world.

❖❖❖❖❖❖❖

When Zen opens its closed fist to show that there is nothing within, spiritual customers are lost. These people enjoy the intoxication of illusion, and, knowing nothing, they recite the scriptures and attend the services with enthusiasm. They are idle dreamers, easily deluded, and their wrongly developed character finds the abrupt system of emancipation difficult to understand.

❖❖❖❖❖❖❖

The one who sees nothing but Mind-Essence is Tathagata himself.
He should be called Avalokitesvara,[16] the one who sees the world clearly with wisdom and compassion.
When one realizes the truth, he knows that karma hindrance does not exist as an entity.
The one who knows not true emptiness worries about debts and credits.

[16] Avalokitesvara . . . the Buddha of Compassion; Chinese: Kwan-yin; Japanese: Kwannon.

Once you realize that nothing exists, everything being the manifestation of Mind-Essence, which is also free of being and non-being, you are Tathagata, the Enlightened One.

The enlightened one has to pay his karmic debts just as anyone else does, but he does not worry about them nor does he contract new debts.

> The hungry man refuses the royal feast;
> How can the ill be cured when they turn from the
> good physician?

Is your hunger satisfied when another eats? Is your thirst quenched when another drinks? Are you rested when another sleeps? By whose efforts will you be enlightened?

❖❖❖❖❖❖❖

> If you have the wisdom of prajna, you can practice
> Zen in the world of desires.
> Like the lotus unconsumed by the fire, nothing
> can destroy your Zen.
> Although Yuse, a monk, once broke the main pre-
> cepts, he went ahead, without faltering, to reach
> Nirvana;
> The pure land, which he built, exists even now.
> Buddha-Dhamma makes anyone fearless.
> What a pity that stupid minds do not appreciate
> this fact!
> They consider only the loss or gain within the
> precepts
> Forgetting that they can still open the secret door
> of Tathagata unaided.
> In ages past two monks broke the precepts.
> Their chief monk, Upali, considered them hopeless
> in the light of his feeble understanding,

But Vimalakirti, a layman, cleared their clouds of
doubt to realize truth as frost is melted in the
warm sunshine.

A Zen student must pass through the world of desires. In India
a story is told of a lotus flower that bloomed in the midst of fire.
Like the lotus or like the phoenix a Zen student will rise from
the ashes of his worldly desires and vain regrets never turning
from his course toward enlightenment. He will pay his karmic
debts without question. The frost of his doubt is melted by the
warm sunshine of realization that illumines all beings.

The wonderful power of emancipation!
It is applied in countless ways . . . in limitless ways.
One should make four kinds of offering for this
    treasure.
If you mean to pay for it, a million gold pieces are
    not enough;
If you sacrifice everything you have, it will not
    cover your debt.
A few words from your realization are payment in
    full, even for debts of the remote past.

Some sincere students meditate morning and evening and at
any other leisure moment to attain emancipation. You have
studied other religions and schools of philosophy hoping to free
yourself from entanglement, and some of these have taken a part
of your familiar burden only in exchange for their own creeds
and dogmas. You must throw them all off at once!

Buddhism takes away your unnecessary burdens but gives you
nothing in return. If you think you have attained anything in

this Zen-do, drop it at the gate and go home with empty hands. There you will find yourself in an atmosphere of peace . . . this is your power of emancipation.

The four kinds of offering are clothes, bedding, food and medicine. These are always given to a monk, but any man, who has the power of emancipation, owes his happiness not only to monks or teachers but to mankind and all sentient beings.

> Zen, superior among all teachings, is the Dharma
>   king,
> As is proven by the attainment of countless Tatha-
>   gatas.
> Now I know what the Mani-gem is,
> I transmit it to anyone who receives it accordingly.

Although there is nothing to be termed great or small in prajna, all people cherish comparative thoughts until they are enlightened; therefore, Yoka-daishi says that the innumerable Tathagatas prove that Zen provides the most direct route to wisdom for those who are strong enough to undertake this path. Even though most people will avoid this steep, rocky course, those who follow it make the choice themselves . . . they are not chosen by a god, they are not accidentally a member of a favored race, nation or creed. Such superficialities have nothing to do with Zen. Each of you may become a Bodhisattva.

> In the eye of realization there is nothing to be seen.
> There is neither man nor Buddha;
> All things in the universe are mere bubbles on the
>   sea.
> Sages and wise men disappear in a lightning flash.

Jews and Christians find it difficult to erase the idea of a god separate from man; although Buddhists know that Gautama Buddha was once a person like themselves, most of them cherish the idea of becoming a Buddha only in some future life. All are caught in the web of dualism, wisdom and ignorance. Whatever you see, hear, smell, taste or think, are the phenomena of your subjectivity and objectivity. No matter how subtle or refined these phenomena may be, Zen insists that you cannot attain enlightenment as long as you are the slave of your dualistic attachment.

❖❖❖❖❖❖❖

Even at the moment of the fatal blow,
A Zen student keeps his equanimity as usual.
He carries his meditation moment after moment.
Nothing in the world can put out his lamp of
    wisdom.
The sun may turn cold and the moon hot,
But even then
No devils or satans can crush
The ultimate truth of Buddha-Dhamma.
As the elephant draws the carriage,
The great wheels are turned.
Can the road be blocked by a foolish mantis
    stretching his legs?

❖❖❖❖❖❖❖

A tyrannical king of China once killed a Buddhist monk who refused to marry the royal princess. At the last moment the monk said:

"These groups of four elements have not belonged to me from the beginning. The five skandhas[17] deceived you, giving you the illusion of a body. Your sword may as well cut off my head as this spring breeze blows the blossoms from the tree."

[17] Skandhas: form (rupam); sensation or sense-perception (vedana); thought (samjna); conformation (samskara); consciousness (vijnana).

Zen offers no miracle to save your life at the last moment, but it can give you equanimity at all times. Just train yourselves in meditation to shut off both your subjectivity and your objectivity. Then you can shut off your subjectivity and melt into your objectivity, or shut off your objectivity and live in your subjectivity. When you can open both your subjectivity and your objectivity carrying your day's work smoothly and happily, you will be living in Zen. The teaching of Buddha is too simple, so people hesitate to practice it.

The "great wheels" are Buddha-Dhamma, and the elephant is enlightenment. In China the mantis has always symbolized a person who overestimates his power. Like a teacher who juggles the ancient names derived from religion and philosophy seeking to block the road to independent thought, the mantis stretches his legs, but the elephant-drawn carriage rolls on.

The elephant is not found in the company of rabbits.
Enlightenment transcends meager intellection.
Stop looking at the skies with a pipe;
Heavens exist beyond your measurement.
There remains nothing but your own actualization.
Come to me this minute and deal with me personally.

Fragmentary Notes
of Bodhi-Dharma's Disciples*

Question: What is Buddha-Mind?

Answer: Your mind is it. When you see the self-same essence of it, you can call it suchness. When you see the changeless nature of it, you can call it Dharmakaya. It does not belong to anything; therefore, it is called Emancipation. It works easily and freely, being never disturbed by others; therefore, it is called the True Path. It was not born, and, therefore, it is not going to perish, so it is called Nirvana.

Comment: That mind is not yours. It is a constituent of all sentient beings' minds. You simply call it yours and others' as children play at being grown up.

Question: What is Tathagata?

Answer: One who knows that he comes from nowhere and goes nowhere.

Question: What is Buddha?

Answer: One who realizes the truth, and holds nothing that is to be realized.

---

* Early in the twentieth century M. A. Stein excavated some manuscripts from Tung Huang, among which were some notes gathered by Bodhi-Dharma's disciples. These were placed in the National Library of Pei-ping, China, where Dr. D. T. Suzuki copied them, later having them published in Japan in 1933.

Nyogen Senzaki received a copy of the book from which he translated the following notes into English. They consist of a question by a disciple, and the answer by Bodhi-Dharma, and, in many cases, a comment by Nyogen Senzaki.

Comment: Buddha said to Subhuti, "What do you think? In ancient times when the Tathagata was with Dipanakara Buddha, did he have attainment in the Dharma?" Subhuti answered, "No, World-honored One, he did not. The Tathagata while with Dipanakara Buddha had no attainment whatever in the Dharma." Bodhi-Dharma was certainly the twenty-eighth successor of Buddha Sakyamuni.

Question: What is Dharma?

Answer: It was never produced, and will never be reduced; therefore, it is called Dharma, the norm of the universe.

Question: What is Sangha?

Answer: It is so named because of the beauty of its harmony.

Comment: We learn nothing but to form a true Sangha . . . harmony of one to another, and harmony of mind and body.

❖❖❖❖❖❖❖

Question: What is meditation in emptiness?

Answer: One observes things in the phenomenal world, yet always dwells in emptiness. That is meditation in emptiness.

Comment: Zen-Getsu was a descendant of Bodhi-Dharma who lived in China during the Tang Dynasty. As though he wished to illustrate Bodhi-Dharma's words, he said, "Living in the world yet not clinging to nor forming attachments for the dust of the world, is the way of the true Zen student." Many Buddhists are like those three monkeys that shut their eyes, ears and mouths so as not to see, hear or speak evil. They are afraid to face things in the phenomenal world. Instead of dwelling in emptiness, they build their houses on the sand.

Question: How can one dwell in Dharma?

Answer: One should stay neither in in-dwelling Dharma nor in non-dwelling Dharma. He should live naturally in Dharma. This is what you call dwelling in Dharma.

Comment: If you think you are a Zen student, you are labeling yourself unnecessarily. If you call yourself a non-Zen student, you are denying your privilege and forcing yourself off the path. Just live in Zen naturally beyond all self-recognition. This is what you call dwelling in Dharma.

Question: How can a man live as not-man and a woman as not-woman?

Answer: There is no difference in Buddha-nature between a man and a woman, nor an entity designated as man or woman. Physical matter produces the grass and trees as it does human beings. In comparison you say "grass" or "trees." You give all sorts of names to your illusions. Buddha said, "If one sees that everything exists as an illusion, he can live in a higher sphere than ordinary man."

Comment: Zen is not taking the side of either feminism or misogyny. Man and woman are alike Buddha. Only in illusion they appear differently.

Question: If one attains the Nirvana of an arhat, has he Zen realization?

Answer: He is just dreaming and so are you.

Comment: Just like Bodhi-Dharma! Did you hear what he said?

Question: If one practices the six paramitas, and passes through the ten stages of Bodhisattvahood, and completes ten thousand virtues, he should know that all things are not born, therefore, they are not going to perish. Such realization is neither intuition nor intellectuality. He has nothing to receive and there is nothing to receive him. Has this man Zen realization?

Answer: He is just dreaming and so are you.

Question: If a man has ten powers, and accomplishes four forms of fearlessness, and completes eighteen systems of the teaching, he is the same as Buddha who attained enlightenment under the pippala tree. He can save all sentient beings and then enter into Nirvana. Is he not a real Buddha?

Answer: He is just dreaming and so are you.

Question: I have heard that all Buddhas in the past, present and future preached the same Dharma and countless beings were saved from suffering. Is it not true?

Answer: You have heard someone speak of dreams, and you yourself are actually dreaming. Whatever you figure with your dualistic mind never makes a true account of mind essence, therefore, I call you a dreamer. Dream is one thing and realization another. Do not mix them together. Wisdom in the dream is not the real wisdom. One who has true wisdom does not hold self-recognition. Buddhas in the past, present and future are in the realm beyond cognition. If you shut off your thinking faculty, blocking off the road of your mind, you will enter a different sphere. Until that time, whatever you think, whatever you say, whatever you do is nothing but foolishness in dreamland.

Comment: What are the six paramitas? What are the ten stages of Bodhisattvahood? What are the ten thousand virtues? What are the ten powers? What are the four forms of fearlessness? What are the eighteen systems of teaching? When you travel by plane do you recite the name of each city, town or whistle stop over which you pass? Zen demands that you start without hesitation, proceeding to your destination quickly and directly. Bodhi-Dharma is calling you. Why don't you wake up!

Question: What kind of wisdom should one use to cut off delusions?

Answer: When you observe your delusions, you will know that they are baseless and not dependable. In this way you can cut confusion and doubt. This is what I call wisdom.

Comment: A Zen student should not fear delusions. He should gaze at them squarely and determine their true nature. A Japanese poem says, "The real form of the ghost was nothing but a group of withered reeds in the late autumn field."

Question: What sort of delusions will be cleared by Zen?

Answer: Any delusions of mediocrity, of a philosopher, of a Çravaka, of a Pratyeka-Buddha, or of a Bodhisattva.

Comment: Bodhi-Dharma thinks that all these people should wash their faces in the cold water of Zen.

Question: What is the difference between a sage's most excellent life and the common people's everyday life?

Answer: It is like gossamer. Some mistake it for vapor, but it is in fact a spider's silk that floats in the air. A mediocre person sees the sage's life, and believes it to be the same as his own everyday life; whereas the enlightened man sees the holy path in a life of mediocrity. You will observe in the sutras that all Buddhas preach for two groups . . . the mediocre and the wise, but in the eye of Zen, a sage's life is one of mediocrity and the mediocre person's as the sage's. This one life has no form and is empty by nature. If you become attached to any form, you should reject it. If you see an ego, a soul, a birth or a death, reject them all.

Question: Why and how do we reject them?

Answer: If you have Zen, you should not see a thing. The *Tao-Teh-Ching* says, "The most firmly established in the path appears the most remiss."

Comment: Zen is the offspring of Buddhism and Taoism. Bodhi-Dharma refers to the forty-first section of the *Tao-Teh-Ching*: "The superior man, as soon as he hears of the path, earnestly practices the teaching; the average man, hearing of the path, sometimes remembers it and sometimes forgets it; the inferior man, hearing of the path, ridicules it. The teaching of the path resembles a deep valley; the most innocent appears to be most ashamed; the highest in the virtues appears to be the humblest; the most firmly established in the path appears the most remiss; the finest instrument is the latest to be perfected; the largest bell sounds rarely. The path is unseen and inscrutable, nevertheless, it is precisely this path that alone can give and accomplish."

Question: What do you call the mind of greediness?
Answer: It is the mind of ignorance.

Question: What do you call the mind of egolessness?
Answer: It is the mind of Çravaka, Buddha's actual disciple.

Question: What do you call the mind of no-entity?
Answer: It is the mind of sages who have no connection with the teaching of Buddha, but discover the truth of no-entity by themselves.

Question: What do you call the mind which has no particular understanding, and also no painful delusions?
Answer: It is the mind of Bodhisattvas.

Question: What do you call the mind which has nothing to know and also nothing to realize?
Answer: No answer from Bodhi-Dharma.

Bodhi-Dharma said, "Dharmakaya has no form, therefore, one sees it without seeing. Dharma has no voice; therefore, one hears it without hearing. Prajna has nothing to be known; therefore, one knows it without knowing. If he thinks that he is seeing, he sees it incompletely. If he thinks that he knows it, he does not know it thoroughly. When he knows it without knowing, he knows it completely. If one does not know this, he is not a true knower. If one thinks that he is gaining, he is not gaining entirely. When he gains non-gaining, he owns everything. If one thinks that he is right, his righteousness is not perfect. When he transcends right and wrong, his virtues are accomplished. Such wisdom is the gate-opener to a hundred thousand gates of the higher wisdom."

Comment: Although these recorded teachings of Bodhi-Dharma were lost in the caves of Tung Huang more than thirteen hundred years, Zen students continued to live as he taught. The lamp of Dharma still burns, proving that wisdom itself is untransmissible and only to be obtained by living.

There is a Zen poem written by a remote descendant of Bodhi-Dharma:

When the soft rain moistens my clothes,
I see the Buddha without seeing.
When a petal of a flower falls quietly,
I hear the voice of the patriarch without hearing.

"See Dharma-kaya without seeing." Dharma-kaya is nothing but your own true self, if I express it ethically. As a religious term it is called "Buddha-kaya," and, philosophically, "Dharma-kaya." Haku-in says, "It is the sound of one hand," and this wandering monk in America declares it is the single eye of which Meister Eckhart has spoken. Never mind the names! It is neither knowable nor unknowable. Just see it without seeing, hear it without hearing, and gain it without gaining. Bodhi-Dharma mentions the hundred thousand gates of wisdom. Do not count them. If you do, you will be imprisoned. Tell your great-great-grandfather they are all gateless gates in dream land.

❖❖❖❖❖❖❖

Said Bodhi-Dharma, "All Buddhas preach emptiness. Why? Because they wish to crush the concrete ideas of the students. If a student even clings to an idea of emptiness, he betrays all Buddhas. One clings to life although there is nothing to be called life; another clings to death although there is nothing to be called death. In reality there is nothing to be born, consequently, there is nothing to perish.

"By clinging one recognizes a thing or an idea. Reality has neither inside, outside, nor middle part. An ignorant person creates delusions and suffers from discrimination. Right and wrong do not exist in reality. An ignorant person creates them, recognizes them, near or far, inward or outward. He then suffers from discrimination. This is the general way of the phenomenal world."

Comment: When I was a child, my foster father gave me my first lesson in emptiness. He used to keep all sweets in a box, passing it to me occasionally when I would ask him if there was anything in it. One day he answered, "This time there is nothing but emptiness." "May I please have that emptiness?" I asked. My foster father answered, "My dear child, emptiness has no form, no color. It has no sound, no odor. You cannot taste it in your mouth. You cannot touch it with your hand. It did not enter this box, and it will not go out of the box. It is neither good nor bad. It is neither pretty nor ugly. It is neither heavy nor light. I know that you will neither like it nor dislike it. Now look and see!" He then took off the cover of the box. At the time I knew only that there was no sweet in the box; the meaning of his words was beyond my comprehension. It took me more than ten years of

study and Zen meditation to realize the true meaning of emptiness. The words of Bodhi-Dharma may not be clear to you, but
be patient and wait until you actually experience it. These words
hold the brilliancy of the lamp of Dharma. I hope that you all
will devote yourselves to constant meditation and discover the
light that will illumine not only yourselves, but all sentient
beings in the world.

Bodhi-Dharma said to his disciples, "The teaching of Buddha
gives you the highest wisdom. No one can describe it without
experience. Generation after generation all patriarchs worked
hard for it. None of them wasted time for foolish things. They
practiced what the ordinary man cannot practice. They bore
what the common people cannot bear. If you have some virtues
and knowledge of the world, do not be conceited about them.
With such petty attainment how can you turn the wheel of
Dharma of the Mahayana teaching?"

If you American students carry the spirit of this saying, you
need not depend upon the trash excavated at Tung Huang. Just
go straight ahead to the palace of your own innerliness and meet
the blue-eyed monk face to face.

Question: Are there fast and slow ways of attainment?

Answer: If one sees that endless time is the mind, he will attain
quickly, but if he makes a point in his mind and aims at his
destination, he will attain slowly. The wise one knows his mind
is the path; the stupid one makes a path beyond his mind. He
does not know where the path is nor does he know that mind
itself is the path.

Comment: Whoever recorded these sayings of Bodhi-Dharma
must have had slow reaction time. For present American students
the first two sentences are more than enough. One does not
punch a time clock twice upon arrival.

Question: Why does one attain quickly?

Answer: Because mind is the body of the path, therefore, is quickly reached. Stupid ones mark their own time starting according to that standard, therefore, they must make their own destination according to their own delusions.

Comment: For instance, if one wants to enjoy his life, he can do it wherever he is whenever he feels like it. If he aims at something to be acquired, he must have created his own destination using his concept of time and place. With the addition of two more delusions he cannot enjoy his life thoroughly.

Question: What part of the mind is the body of the path?

Answer: Mind is like the wood or stone from which a person carves an image. If he carves a dragon or a tiger, and seeing it fears it, he is like a stupid person creating a picture of hell and then afraid to face it. If he does not fear it, then his unnecessary thoughts will vanish. Part of the mind produces sight, sound, taste, odor and sensibility, and from them raises greed, anger and ignorance with all their accompanying likes and dislikes. Thus is planted the seed, which grows to great suffering. If one realizes that from the beginning mind essence is empty and quiet, he should know no specific time or place. Instead he makes an image of a tiger, lion, dragon, demon, warrior or other monster, recognizes them by comparison and produces likes and dislikes. If he knows that from the beginning there is no such thing, then he should know that mind essence is not formed, therefore, these images are nothing but illusions. When he realizes this fact, he will be emancipated at that instant.

Question: What is the natural, simple mind, and what is the artificial, complicated mind?

Answer: Letters and speeches come from the artificial, complicated mind. Both in the material and immaterial world a person stays or goes, sits or lies down, and moves innocently, or, it can be said, in the natural, simple mind. When one remains unmoved by pleasure or suffering, his mind may be called the natural, simple mind.

Question: What is right and what is wrong?

Answer: Discrimination with no-mind is right. Discrimination with mind is wrong. When one transcends right and wrong, he is truly right. In a Sutra it says, "When one dwells on the right road, he does not discriminate, 'this is right, this is wrong.' "

Comment: "With mind" means with self-centered, psychological movement. "With no-mind" means unhampered, natural, selfless movement.

Question: What is a sagacious student, and what is a dull student?

Answer: A sagacious student does not depend on his teacher's words, but uses his own experience to find the truth. A dull student depends on coming to a gradual understanding through his teacher's word. A teacher has two kinds of students; one hears the teacher's words without clinging to the material nor to the immaterial, without attaching to form or to non-form, without thinking of animate objects or of inanimate objects . . . this is the sagacious student; the other, who is avid for understanding, accumulates meanings, and mixes good and bad, is the dull student. The sagacious student understands instantly; he does not raise inferior mind when he hears the teaching, nor does he follow the sage's mind, he transcends both wisdom and ignorance. Even though one hears the teaching and does not cling to worldly desires, does not love Buddha or the true path, if, when he has to select one out of two, he selects quietness from confusion, wisdom from ignorance, inactivity from activity and clings to one or the other of these, then he is a dull student. If one transcends both wisdom and ignorance, has no greed for the teaching, does not live in right recollectedness, does not raise right thinking, and does not have aspirations to be Pratyeka Buddha nor Bodhisattva, then he is a sagacious student.

Suggestions for Zen Students
by
Zen-Getsu*

Living in the world, yet not clinging to or forming attachments for the dust of the world, is the way of a true Zen student.

Witnessing the good actions of another person, encourage yourself to follow his example. Hearing of the mistaken action of another person, advise yourself not to emulate it.

Even though you are alone in a dark room conduct yourself as though you were facing a noble guest.

Express your feelings, but never become more expressive than your true nature.

Poverty is your treasure. Do not exchange it for an easy life.

A person may look like a fool and yet not be stupid. He may be conserving his wisdom and guarding it carefully.

The virtues are the fruits of self-discipline, and do not drop from heaven of themselves like rain or hail.

Modesty is the foundation of all virtues. Let your neighbors find you before you make yourself known to them.

A noble heart never forces itself forward. Its words are as rare gems seldom displayed.

Every day is a fortunate day for a true student. Time passes but he never lags behind.

Neither glory nor shame can move his heart.

Do not discuss right or wrong. Always censure yourself, never another.

Some things, although right, were considered wrong for many generations. Since the value of righteousness may be recognized after centuries, there is no need to crave immediate appreciation.

Why do you not leave everything to the great law of the universe and pass each day with a peaceful smile?

---

* The biography of Zen-getsu is unknown except that he was a student of Toku-san (782-865) and Seki-So (807-888).

GLOSSARY

Asamskrita: not subject to causation, the world of birthlessness and deathlessness.

Avalokitesvara: the Buddha of Compassion; Chinese: Kwan-yin; Japanese: Kwannon.

Bodhisattva: a person dedicated not only to his own enlightenment but also to the enlightenment of all sentient beings.

Buddha-Dhamma: Pali for Buddha-Dharma, Sanskrit: enlightened wisdom.

Buddha-Hrydaya: brilliancy of enlightenment.

Buddha Sakyamuni: the same as Gautama Buddha.

Dharma: Sanskrit; Dhamma, Pali; the content of enlightenment to be realized intuitively, directly, and personally experienced.

Dharmakaya: same as Dharma-body; the Law body of the Buddha; original man in full; the sound of one hand; the eternal Buddha.

Dhyana: Sanskrit . . . meditation.

Hinayana: Small Vehicle, one of the two main groups of Buddhists.

Karma: the law of cause and effect.

Ko-an: a problem given to a student for solution.

Mahayana: Great Vehicle, one of the two main groups of Buddhists.

Nidana: process of Karma relation.

Nirvana: synonymous with enlightenment, but is not the negative condition as translated by many scholars, nor is it a condition of non-existence, nor to be found outside of Samsara.

Prajna: that condition of the ability to see directly into the true nature of things beyond mere intellection.

Prajnaparamita: the sixth precept, or practice of wisdom.

Samadhi: Is sometimes used in place of dhyana, but more often is referred to as that condition achieved by the practice of dhyana.

Samatha: quietude.

Samsara: world of birth and death.

Samskrita: subject to causation, the world of birth and death.

San-zen: from Chinese *San-Ch'an,* to study Zen, especially the examination of a student by a teacher.

Sastras or Shastras: commentaries on the Sutras.

Tathagata: Buddha, Mind-Essence, Eternal Presence, Eternal Now.

Tripitaka: literally, Three Baskets. All the Buddhist scriptures as a unit.

Tathagata-dhyana: enlightened meditation.

Vipassana: contemplation or discernment (Tendai School).

Za-zen: from the Chinese, *tso ch'an,* to sit in meditation.

SUGGESTED READING

Suzuki, Daisetz Teitaro
  Essays in Zen Buddhism, First Series. Rider & Co., 1949.
  Essays in Zen Buddhism, Second Series. Rider & Co., 1950.
  Essays in Zen Buddhism, Third Series. Luzac & Co., 1934.
  The Zen Doctrine of No-Mind. Philosophical Library, 1949.
  The Training of the Zen Buddhist Monk. Eastern Buddhist
    Society, Kyoto, 1934.
  Living by Zen. Sanseido Publishing Co., Tokyo, 1949.
  The Lankavatara Sutra. Routledge & Sons, Ltd., 1932.
  Studies in the Lankavatara Sutra. Routledge & Sons, Ltd.,
    1930.
  Introduction to Zen Buddhism. Eastern Buddhist Society,
    Kyoto, 1934.
  Manual of Zen Buddhism. Rider & Co., 1950.
Nyogen Senzaki and Paul Reps
  101 Zen Stories. David McKay Company, Philadelphia.

INDEX

Aladdin, 57
Allah, 11
Anatta, 25; 39
Anicca, 25; 39
Apo, 38
Asamskrita, 51, 51fn
Attainment body, 44
Avalokitesvara, 67, 67 fn

Bodhi-Dharma, 3; 4; 21, 61, 73, 74, 76, 77, 78, 79, 80, 81
Bodhisattva, 17, 18fn, 47, 59, 70, 77, 78, 84
Brahma, 11
Brahmajala Sutra, 13
Buddha, death of 3; Gautama, 8, 44, 71; Sakayamuni, 4, 4fn, 20, 21, 51, 53; Oriental god, 9; meaning of, 11, 73; state of mind, 20, 27; eternal, 32; realization, 37; three bodies of, 43, 44; countless, 48; wisdom, 54; revelation of, 58; prophecy, 63; 76
Buddhacitta, 28
Buddha-Dhamma, 54, 72
Buddha-Dharma, 23, 23fn, 68, 71
Buddhahood, 12, 20, 58
Buddha-Hrydaya, 24
Buddhakaya, 79
Buddha-Mind, 73
Buddha-nature, 31, 40, 49, 53, 62, 75
Buddhism, in China, 3, 4; two schools, 3; and Taoism, 5; contemporary, 8; mind, 11; first cause, 11; future life, 12; attitude to other religions, 13; spread of, 14; way to emancipation, 20; other sects of, 46; religion of reason, 48; view of emptiness, 55; teaching of self-enlightenment, 61; three processes of, 63; accumulating terms, 66; removes burdens, 69
Buddhists, belief in god, 10; 71, 74

Causation, law of, 45, 63
Ch'an, 5
Chandana, 64, 64fn
Christians, 13, 56, 71
Compassion, 48
Confucianism, 3, 4, 56, 66
Çravaka, 59, 66, 77, 78

Dana, 35
Dai-to, 15
David, 42
Deva, 35
Dhamma, 9, 62, 63, 64
Dhammapada, 20
Dharma, 5, 9, 29, 50, 51, 52, 70, 74, dwelling in, 75; 79
Dharmabody, 32, 32fn; 44
Dharmakaya, 31, 31fn; 44, 59, 72, 79
Dhyana, 5, 5fn, 15, Patriarch's, 35
Diamond Sutra, 18
Dipankara Buddha 51, 51fn, 74
Dō-gen, 23
Dukkha, 39

Einstein, 10
Eki-do, 17
Eloquence, four kinds of, 48
Emancipation, eight sorts, 43, 44; 45, 52, 55, 73
Emptiness, 19, 44

Gateless Gate, 38
Gautama Siddhartha, 9, 12
Gen-kaku, 28, 29, 30
Gen-saku, 28, 29
God, 10, 11, 17

Haku-in, 36, 79
Hinayana, 3, 3fn, 8, 44
Hui-k'e, 4
Hui-neng, 28

89